All Things Bright and Beautiful

A Comedy

Keith Waterhouse and Willis Hall

Samuel French–London
New York–Sydney–Toronto–Hollywood

All Things Bright and Beautiful

This play was first produced in London, at the Phoenix Theatre, on 13th December 1962, with the following cast:

DESMOND COOPER	.. ..	*Griffith Davies*
DEANNA HESSELTINE	.. ..	*Juliet Cooke*
CHARLES HESSELTINE	.. ..	*Jack Smethurst*
BALOO ..	.. ..	*Eileen Kennally*
OLD JAKIE	.. ..	*Dermot Kelly*
QUEENIE HESSELTINE	.. ..	*Peggy Mount*
ALBERT HESSELTINE	.. ..	*John Barrie*
HARRY LAUDER HESSELTINE	.. ..	*Brian Peck*
DOUGLAS DOBSON	.. ..	*Ken Parry*

The play was directed by VAL MAY *with décor by* ALAN BARRETT

The scene is the kitchen/living-room of the Hesseltine house and also in the communal yard outside.

ACT ONE
A Friday evening

ACT TWO
The following morning

ACT THREE
Late the same afternoon

No reference is intended in this play, to any person, alive or dead.

NOTE: *Running time of this play, excluding intervals, is approximately one hour and forty-five minutes.*

CHARACTERS

DEANNA HESSELTINE	19, a girl of rough spirit who has learned to keep her emotions well hidden.
DESMOND COOPER	19, who like any boy of his age is interested in very little except sex.
CHARLES HESSELTINE	25, already a confirmed bachelor, slovenly and dourly shy.
BALOO	In her early thirties, a short intense woman who, although a member of the working-class herself, feels herself to have a broader vision.
QUEENIE HESSELTINE	In her mid-forties, a woman hardened in the life-long fight for minor luxuries such as a drink on a Saturday night.
ALBERT HESSELTINE	In his late forties, a man sure of himself and not given to self-criticism.
HARRY LAUDER HESSELTINE	23, probably the pleasantest member of the family and certainly the most communicable.
OLD JAKIE	In his seventies, a useless old man who has grown sycophantic and servile in his dependence on the people around him.
DOUGLAS DOBSON	In his early forties, a man alive to his responsibilities as the representative of bureaucracy.

Printed in Great Britain by offset lithography by
Billings & Sons Ltd, Worcester

PRODUCTION NOTE

All Things Bright and Beautiful is a comedy with serious implications, and the success of any production that is to bring out these implications will depend largely upon the director's technique in preventing the meaning of the play from being sunk in a morass of comic business. The plight of the Hesseltine family is a very real one and the play should be approached as the story of a family faced with the indignities of having to depend on a petty bureaucracy for happiness and even the essentials of life. It is *not* a farce about a bunch of layabouts who acquire a church lectern.

In casting, costume and production the director should think carefully about the Hesseltines as a family unit before he considers them singly. It will be apparent that, although the family lives in a slum house, four of its members are in full employment; consequently we are not dealing with a household struck by poverty. Their manners and behaviour may be slovenly but they are presentably dressed. Their home is uncared for, not because they can't afford to refurnish it but, because they have grown sick of and uncaring about its basic tawdriness. The Welfare State is real for them but it exists in the world some miles away—we find them huddled on top of each other in a street which they recognize as a relic of the past. They squabble and quarrel among themselves like most families although perhaps a little more frequently than most because of their cramped living conditions. If they were ever to obtain their Utopian semi-detached they would no doubt settle down quite happily and enjoy the normal, everyday bickering of normal, everyday folk. The director should remember this and sternly hold in check any attempts by his cast to turn the Hesseltines into a kind of Casey's court with everybody constantly at everybody else's throat. The point that this is more or less a normal family living in unnatural if not unusual conditions will be best brought out during the brief moments of family unity—moments when we see that basically Queenie *does* care deeply and strongly about her family and that they in turn care about her.

Perhaps the main difficulty of the production—certainly from the point of view of the actors—is that the two main characters in the story are an inanimate lectern and an invisible small boy. The three curtains belong to these two scene stealers; the Act One curtain and the final curtain are shared by them. It is up to the director to decide which of them is to hold the audience's attention when the curtain falls and how his actors should be grouped in relation to this area of interest. In the London production at the end of the first act, the cast turned their attention back to the lectern at the moment Queenie grabbed the shoe and went upstairs, and the curtain was held back until she had actually entered Rory's bedroom, which was visible in the set. Thus, at the moment the curtain fell, everybody onstage was looking at the lectern and consequently so was the audience. The effect achieved was that at the end of the first act one saw the play as one in which an uncultured family is thinking vaguely and incoherently about the absence of beauty in their lives, rather than as a kitchen comedy in which a small boy gets a good hiding for playing truant from the wolf cubs. On the final curtain the whole family, including Queenie, who was still holding the severed head of the eagle, turned and looked towards the wall beyond which was the lavatory where the invisible Rory was singing. And the effect here was the rejection of the beauty which had been within their grasp and the turning back to the practicalities of living such as half-murdering Rory. The final curtain should be sad and savage.

The lectern is, of course, the most important prop in the play. In the London production there were obviously two lecterns—the one that features in the first and second acts and the half-painted one that features in the third. If the director has an obliging ASM who will stay up every night to repaint the lectern, obviously he can get by with one—but it must be borne in mind that the lectern has got to take a lot of knocking about and dragging backwards and forwards. The head which is to be sawn off nightly must be firmly fixed on yet capable of quickly being sawn off. *

The voice of Rory is another important factor. In the London production experiments were made with a taped voice but it was found more successful to do the voice live off-stage by one of the female members of the cast. The voice should not be comic but should approximate to a schoolboy treble.

The set can be simple or complex according to the means available. It requires basically only the living room and yard with a wall dividing them. In the London production the back wall of the house was cut away to reveal a rather Lowryesque backcloth on which one saw rows and rows of terrace houses and, in the far background, the tall towers of the new Utopia rising up. There was also an open staircase leading up to Rory's bedroom but this can, if necessary, be dispensed with. The living room area should give the impression of cramped quarters while, at the same time, leaving an adequate playing area.

KEITH WATERHOUSE and WILLIS HALL

---

* The lecterns may be hired from Samuel French Ltd. Details available on application.

★ ALL THINGS BRIGHT AND BEAUTIFUL

ACT ONE

The action of the play takes place in the combined living-room and kitchen of the Hesseltine house, and also in the communal yard outside.

The house is at the end of a row of terrace houses and the yard contains three dustbins and three lavatories—each of which is shared by two families. There is a street lamp at the entrance to the yard.

The living-room contains the furniture which was bought when QUEENIE and ALBERT were married twenty-five years ago—and for which they are still paying. There is a rexine three-piece suite, a dining-table and four chairs and a sideboard. The additions since that time have been an enormous television set and stand and an elaborate circular glass-fronted china cupboard. The door leading to the street is at the rear, as is also the window. There is a flight of stairs, right, leading to the bedrooms. Under the stairs is a door leading to the cellar. There is an old-fashioned fireplace with an oven which is no longer in use. There is an old porcelain sink in the rear right-hand corner and also a recently installed modern gas cooker.

> *When the curtain rises the lights in the house are dimmed and the street lamp in the yard is lit. DEANNA HESSELTINE is leaning awkwardly against a wall in the yard, carefully avoiding the dustbins. DESMOND COOPER, her current boy friend, has one hand propped against the wall and is questioning her on her lack of co-operation.*

DESMOND. Right. Well, we know where we are then, don't we? If you won't—you won't.

DEANNA. I've told you I wouldn't.

DESMOND. I know you did. I heard you.

DEANNA. Yes—well—

(*There is a long pause and DESMOND moves away, stuffs his hands in his pockets and leans against a dustbin. His tone becomes academic rather than hopeful.*)

DESMOND. Well, what have I done then?

DEANNA. You haven't done nothing.

DESMOND. I must have done. Else why not?

DEANNA. I don't. I don't do that sort of thing.

DESMOND. I bet you don't.

DEANNA. I don't. And whoever says I do is a liar.

DESMOND. Yeh—well, there must be a lot of liars about.

DEANNA. Yeh—there must be.

(*There is a further pause and* DESMOND *considers the matter.*)

DESMOND. There's two liars in this street.

DEANNA. Well, if one of them's Rex Armistead he is a liar.

DESMOND. Well, that's three then.

DEANNA. 'cause he never got nowhere near it. He wants to get off his knees first. I've been to the pictures with him twice, that's all. We went to the Crescent one night to see *The Unforgotten*—that was once—and we went to the Tivoli the other. I can't remember what we saw now.

DESMOND (*he again considers*). What about Harry Tempest?

DEANNA. What about him?

DESMOND. Well, what about him?

DEANNA. Don't know what you're on about.

DESMOND. Don't you?

DEANNA. No—I don't.

DESMOND. No, but I do though. What about Frank Monoghan—don't tell me he hasn't?

DEANNA. 'course he hasn't. What do you think I am? (DESMOND *stares at her in disbelief.*) He hasn't! He hasn't.

DESMOND. Yeh, well. . . . I believe you, thousands wouldn't.

DEANNA. Well, I don't care whether you believe me or you don't believe me, it's all the same to me what you flaming do.

(DESMOND, *realizing that this questioning is getting him nowhere, decides to change his tactics. He again props one hand against the wall and the light of battle comes into his eyes.* DEANNA *is immediately on her guard. They size each other up like two adversaries.*)

DESMOND. What time is it?

(DEANNA *glances at her watch.*)

DEANNA. Quarter to . . .

(DESMOND, *seizing the opportunity, makes a sudden lunge to embrace her.* DEANNA *is too quick for him, however, and roughly grabs his hand.*)

(*Without rancour.*) You're not quick enough—are you?

DESMOND (*innocently*). What? I wasn't doing anything?

DEANNA. You're not going to do anything either.

DESMOND. You never know till you've tried, do you?

DEANNA. Anyway, what we stuck out here for? (*Shivering elaborately.*) It's clap cold stood out here.

DESMOND. You don't want to go in yet, do you? Quarter to ten?

DEANNA. Don't want to stop out here. (*Offhandedly referring to the dustbins.*) Anyway, it stinks out here—always has done.

DESMOND. Well, you're not going in, are you?

DEANNA. 'course I am. I'm starving. I've only had that plate of chips when I came out of work.

DESMOND. Well, that's not my fault—it's your fault.

DEANNA. I don't mind whose fault it is, I'm still hungry. I'm going to have a cup of tea if nothing else. (*Glancing at him.*) You can come in, if you want.

DESMOND. I don't want to come in. What do I want to come in for?

DEANNA. Why not? There's nobody in. There's only our Charles in. You know him.

DESMOND. Well, why can't we stop out here?

DEANNA (*making a move*). You can stop out here, but I know where I'm going. I'm going in. Come on, we can always go out again.

> (DEANNA *forces the issue by moving up the yard to the street at the rear.* DESMOND *follows her reluctantly. They move out of sight as the lights fade down in the yard and simultaneously the lights fade up in the living-room.* CHARLES HESSELTINE *is sitting in an armchair in his stockinged feet.* CHARLES *has a pile of old newspapers and greyhound form-books on the floor beside him. He holds a pencil and paper and is engrossed in his studies.* DEANNA *enters followed by* DESMOND, *who remains by the door.* CHARLES *does not in any way acknowledge their entrance.*)

(*Crossing to the sink to fill the kettle.*) Where's our Rory? Is he in bed?

CHARLES (*without looking up*). You what?

DEANNA. Is our Rory in bed?

CHARLES. I don't know. What you asking me for?

DEANNA (*filling the kettle and turning to* DESMOND). Come in. Take your coat off.

> (DESMOND *moves hesitantly into the room.* DEANNA *indicates* CHARLES, *who has still not looked up.*)

Don't take any notice of him.

> (DESMOND *moves right into the room and, after removing a pile of comics and a pair of shoes from the sofa, perches uneasily on the space that he has cleared.*)

DESMOND (*stiltedly*). Now then.

> (CHARLES *acknowledges* DESMOND's *greeting with a reluctant grunt.*)

DEANNA (*without rancour*). Don't look up when people come in, will you?

CHARLES (*still engrossed in his book*). Shur-rup!

> (DEANNA *places the kettle on the gas ring.*)

DEANNA. Why don't you take your coat off?

DESMOND. I'm all right.

DEANNA. Well, look as though you're stopping.

DESMOND (*pointedly*). We're not stopping, are we? I thought we were supposed to be going out again?

DEANNA (*taking her own coat off*). Give us chance to get in, lad. (*She tosses her coat on to the sofa.*) I know what I'm going to have. I'm going to have some dripping and bread. (*She takes a coronation mug from a shelf above the sink and a sliced loaf which stands permanently on the draining-board.*) Do you want some?

DESMOND. No. I'll just have a cup of tea.

DEANNA (*crossing and holding the mug under* DESMOND's *nose*). It's pork dripping, you know. It isn't beef dripping.

DESMOND. I'm going to have my supper when I get home.

DEANNA. Don't you like dripping?

DESMOND. Yeh—it's all right. I just don't want any.

DEANNA. You don't know what you're missing. (*She crosses to the draining-board and spreads herself a slice of bread and dripping.*) Do you want a slice, our Charles?

CHARLES (*slurring the word*). No.

DEANNA. It's not beef—it's pork. From Sunday's joint.

(CHARLES *does not reply.*)

So do you want some?

CHARLES. Shur-up!

DEANNA (*taking a large bite she speaks through a mouthful of bread and dripping*). I could live on this if I had to.

DESMOND (*noting that* DEANNA *has her mouth full he attempts politely to make conversation with* CHARLES—*indicating the form-books*). Have you got a winner for tomorrow then?

CHARLES (*realizing that he has been spoken to*). You what?

DESMOND (*wishing that he hadn't spoken*). No, I was just looking at your form-books. 'cause your Deanna was saying that you have a bit on every week. Do you make it pay? Do you work for the bookies or do they work for you?

CHARLES (*returning to his studies*). Yeh.

DEANNA (*in an attempt to save the conversation by prolonging it*). He won't tell you. He doesn't tell us, so I'm sure he won't tell you. I've seen him though—coming out of that bookie's on the corner of Back Pemberton Street. He had a fistful of money.

CHARLES. Shur-up, will you!

(DEANNA *does a primitive imitation of* CHARLES *behind his back. This is followed by an awkward silence during which* DEANNA *looks around the room for a new topic of conversation. Her glance falls on*

*a school group photograph on the mantelpiece. She takes down the
photograph and pushes it into* DESMOND'S *reluctant hands.*)

DEANNA. I bet you can't tell which is me out of all these?

DESMOND. What? Is this your class?

DEANNA. Yeh. Was. When we were in standard three. Miss
Hebden's class.

DESMOND. They've coloured it nice, haven't they?

(DEANNA *takes the photograph back from him and studies it.*)

DEANNA. There's hardly one of these girls still lives round here.
(*Pointing.*) She's moved. . . . She's moved. . . . Renee Saunders!
And she must have moved, because she lived in Pottery Fields, and
all that's come down. . . . (*Still pointing.*) That's another who's
moved—she lives up Belle Isle Estate. . . . And you know this
one, don't you?

DESMOND. They all look alike to me. They're all squint-eyed, aren't
they?

DEANNA. Jessie Woollerton! That's another who's in a council house.
Her that I went to see last Sunday. You see you didn't believe me,
did you?

DESMOND. I still don't, love.

DEANNA. I did! For my tea, Sunday afternoon. Hey, and do you
know what they've got in their lavvy? They've got like these blue
tiles right round, and a fitted cabinet with all mirrors.

DESMOND. What do you want mirrors in the closet for?

DEANNA. The bathroom, you daft, dozy idiot! Bathroom cabinet!
For your make-up and Elastoplast and anything like that. (*Excitedly.*)
Hey, I had a bath there! D'you know, if it wasn't so far I'd go up
and have one every week. Because if I'm not sick of dragging that
zinc bath up them cellar steps and getting in after that one! (*She
points at* CHARLES *in disgust. He is deep in his form-books.*)

DESMOND. Well, you'll be in a council house yourself soon, won't
you?

DEANNA (*disbelievingly*). Yes—nineteen-eighty.

(DEANNA *dismisses the subject, returns the photograph to the
mantelpiece and crosses to make the tea. She takes down two cups and
saucers and a mug from the shelf above the sink. She picks up a bottle
containing a small quantity of milk.*)

Did my mam say? Can we use all this milk?

CHARLES. What are you asking me for?

(DEANNA *again does her imitation of* CHARLES. *She takes down
the teapot and proceeds to make tea.*)

DESMOND. Where's your mam and dad? Out?

DEANNA. Where do you think they are? They're not in, are they?

DESMOND. Have they gone out for one?

DEANNA. They'll be down at the Builders Arms tonight.

DESMOND. What? Friday? I thought he was waiting on at the Travellers, Sundays and Fridays?

DEANNA. He's packed it in down there. 'cause this mate of his that used to wait on in the Builders, well, he had to go to hospital. So my dad swopped over. 'cause it's nearer, there's more money, the landlord's better and, of course, he does his own cashing up down there—so, of course, he's better off all round.

DESMOND. Well, he will be, won't he?

DEANNA. And he gets Sunday dinner-times as well, thrown in.

(DEANNA *has now poured out the tea and she crosses, gives* DESMOND *a cup and places the mug beside* CHARLES. CHARLES *glances at the mug, but makes no acknowledgement.*)

DESMOND. 'kyou!

(DEANNA *crosses and picks up her own cup and sits, almost crouching, on a small shoe-box-cum stool by the fireplace.*)

DEANNA (*she sips at her tea for a moment and then glances disapprovingly at the meagre fire*). Call that a fire! You couldn't get up and put some coal on, could you?

CHARLES. Shur-rup!

DEANNA (*to* DESMOND). Honestly! He'd sit there and watch it go out! He would. I've seen him. I come in one cold, freezing night—it's thick with snow. And there's a full bucket of coal there (*pointing to the fireplace*)—a pile of wood in the oven—he's only got to stretch his hand out. But he's sitting there like a tart in a trance trying to warm his hands over two little cinders! Honestly!

CHARLES (*he glances up for the first time*). What's up with you putting some coal on?

DEANNA. Oooh, it can speak! It's a rotten fireplace anyway, is this. 'cause there's that big crack right down the side. But he won't do anything, the landlord.

DESMOND. It's as bad as ours.

DEANNA. If you say anything they tell you they're pulling them down this year. They've been saying that ever since I was at school.

DESMOND. I know. It's like ours. They were condemned in nineteen-twenty-nine, these houses.

DEANNA. They reckon they're going to build flats all round here. Fourteen stories. They've started slum clearance already—down by St. Christopher's. Don't know when they're going to start down here, though.

CHARLES (*again glancing up from his book, his mind still pursuing the subject of the coal*). What's up? You're not paralysed, are you? Can't you pick up a coal bucket now?

(*This effectively kills the conversation and again they lapse into an awkward silence which is broken by knock at the door.*)

DEANNA. Was that our door?

DESMOND. I think so.

(DEANNA *looks puzzled for a moment, and then rises, crosses and opens the door.* BALOO *is standing outside in the street.* DEANNA *stands questioningly looking at* BALOO.)

BALOO. Good evening? I know it's terribly late—I wondered, has Mrs. Hesseltine got a moment?

DEANNA. She's not in. I'm afraid.

CHARLES (*glancing towards the door*). Shut door!

(DEANNA *glances uncertainly, first at* CHARLES *and then at* BALOO.)

DEANNA. Do you want to come in for a minute?

BALOO. Thank you.

(BALOO *enters and* DEANNA *closes the door.* BALOO *is wearing her Assistant Cub Mistress's uniform and is carrying a sheaf of books under her arm.* BALOO *wipes her feet elaborately and remains standing by the door.* DEANNA *crosses and stands in front of the fire.*)

DEANNA. It's cold tonight, isn't it?

BALOO. It is cold. It's cold in that scout hut.

DEANNA (*after a pause*). Well, I don't know what time my mother'll be back.

BALOO. I thought you might all be in bed, but I was just coming back from a meeting and I thought I'd call. I've just been to our District Commissioner's—Mr. Prentice. He only lives up the road.

DEANNA (*politely interested*). Oh, yes?

BALOO. So I had to pass your street. Rory's in bed, I suppose?

DEANNA. Well, I hope he is. Yes. Well, I'm saying he is, I've only just come in myself.

BALOO. I was just wondering if he had a cold. There's a lot of them about.

DEANNA. He looked all right to me when I saw him this morning. (*Turning to* CHARLES.) Is he in bed, our Charles?

CHARLES (*without glancing up*). 'course he's in bed! How many more times!

BALOO. And with him not coming to the Pack Meeting tonight, I just wondered whether he was poorly.

DEANNA. Hasn't he been? He was going, because he asked his mother for threepence for his subs before she went to work this morning.

BALOO. Is Mrs. Hesseltine a working mother, then?

DEANNA (*not understanding and half-belligerent*). How do you mean?

BALOO. We're always interested where there are working mothers.

DEANNA (*ignoring this last*). So didn't our Rory come to the Cubs tonight?

BALOO. Well, no. The whole point is, you see, he's not been for three weeks.

DEANNA. Are you sure?

BALOO. Oh, yes. We've got his absence marked in the register.

DEANNA. Well, the crafty little swine! (BALOO *winces visibly*.) He's been marching off, every week, with his threepence and his little cap and his garter-tabs. I wonder where he's been going. I bet he's been going to the pictures.

BALOO. Well, he's certainly not been to the Pack Meetings.

(BALOO *glances round at a straight-backed chair by the table.* DESMOND, *disinterested, is reading one of* RORY'S *comics which he has found on the sofa*.)

DEANNA. Sit down.

BALOO. Thank you. (*She crosses and sits*.) Because we've been rather disturbed about him for some time. I was having a talk with Bagheera tonight. We both feel that he's a very sensitive boy.

DEANNA (*not understanding*). Who? Our Rory?

BALOO. You see, I didn't know this, but it transpires that Akela probably hurt his feelings the last time he was at the Pack Meeting. You see, he had to reprimand him for making faces during the Grand Howl. Well, of course, it transpires that he wasn't making faces at all —so his sixer tells me. He was just doing his best. He was trying to be a wolf. I feel we owe him an apology.

DEANNA (*still not understanding*). Who? Our Rory?

BALOO. It turns out that Akela reprimanded him rather sharply. And apparently without cause. I was wondering whether he'd got a sense of injustice. Whether that was why he'd stopped coming.

DEANNA. He'll get something when his father hears he hasn't been. And he'll get another clout from my mother for taking that money every week. She'll go bald, she will.

BALOO. We do feel that it's probably our fault. That most probably we're in the wrong. And, of course, he's most probably got a sense of disappointment. You see, he was promised that he was going to be promoted to a second. (*She points to her sleeve*.) You know, one yellow band.

DEANNA. His father'll knock his head clean off his shoulders.

BALOO. I know. It's a great temptation—but, of course, it doesn't solve anything. (*She has been looking at* CHARLES *for some moments and now addresses him*.) Excuse me. (CHARLES *does not look up*.) Excuse me—

DEANNA (*to* CHARLES). There's somebody talking to you, if you did but know it.

CHARLES (*looking up*). You what?

BALOO. I was just saying—you're Charles, aren't you?

CHARLES. Yeh.

BALOO. Yes, I remember your face. You're an old Scout, aren't you?

CHARLES. What.

BALOO (*studying him carefully*). I don't think you were in the Cubs—but you were in the Scouts. You were in the Owl Patrol.

CHARLES (*embarrassed by this conversation*). What.

BALOO. You were in the Owl Patrol when Mr. Bateman was Scout Master. That must be—oh—twelve or thirteen years ago.

CHARLES. What.

BALOO. Don't you remember? I was the lady who was demonstrating the use of the triangular bandage. And you slipped and twisted your ankle when the Troop was playing British Bulldogs. Well, I was the lady who took you to the Infirmary.

CHARLES (*self-consciously*). I don't remember.

(*At this point* CHARLES *refuses to suffer the indignity of this conversation any longer and, bringing it to a close in his usual manner, rises and, form-books in hand, crosses and goes out up the bedroom stairs.* BALOO *watches him go benevolently and turns to* DEANNA.)

BALOO. Oh, yes. I remember him very well.

DEANNA. I can remember him being in the Scouts. Boy Sprouts, we used to say. I was only little, but I can remember. Used to go running down the street after him. Used to shout: "You'll never be a Scout with your shirt hanging out!" And he used to lam out at me with that long pole that they have. I nearly finished up in the Infirmary—never mind him.

BALOO. Well, I'd be grateful if you would mention it to Mrs. Hesseltine—about Rory. See if we can't get it straightened out. Because we don't want to lose him altogether.

DEANNA. He's never in anything for more than five minutes. Lifeboys, he was in that. Chucks out after a fortnight. Sunday school, he goes three weeks. He joined that picture-house club for Saturday mornings, but he has his errands to do. Junior Youth Club—they chucked him out of that, if you ask me anything.

BALOO. Well, we thought he was settling down very nicely with the Pack. (*Going into a set speech on one of her pet subjects.*) Of course, we're only glad that these other organizations do exist. There's very little liaison between us, that's the only snag. And, of course, we are all working for the same end. Keep them off the streets! Occupy them! So, of course, the important thing is not which organization he belongs to—as long as he does belong to one. Although, of course, we would like to feel it was the Cubs.

DEANNA. Well, if he chucks out when my mother's just bought that uniform for him—she'll crucify him, she will.

BALOO (*still pursuing her own train of thought*). Of course, housing, that's another factor. We're losing quite a few of our members now that they've started demolition down near St. Christopher's.

DEANNA. They're supposed to be starting up here.

BALOO. Of course, that was our church. St. Christopher's. I think it's a pity they should pull that church down. It's very old—eighteen something. And, of course, there are all these beautiful carvings. And anybody can walk in. It's left quite unattended. You see, it's what I've been saying. There's so much vandalism. Mrs. Ritchie had to get down on her hands and knees and scrub out hop-scotch marks. Hop-scotch marks! In the aisle of a church! And the lectern, of course. That went today. Well, we don't know whether the workmen have moved it, or someone's been in, or what's happened. And it's a beautiful piece of work. (*Her hands flutter lyrically in the air as she describes the lectern.*) There's the most beautiful eagle and it's hand-carved all the way down—every inch. You've got to see it, but—oh, it's beautiful.

(DESMOND *coughs uncomfortably with boredom.*)

DEANNA (*politely*). Oh, yes.

BALOO. I'm a firm opponent of all forms of corporal punishment, but sacrilege I will not stand for. They should be flogged.

DEANNA. Well, they don't know any better—some of them.

DESMOND (*laying down his comic with an air of finality*). Anyway— (*He rises and stretches elaborately and meaningly.*) I've got to be on my way —very shortly. Very shortly indeed.

BALOO. Yes, well, I shall have to go. (*She glances at her watch.*)

DEANNA (*speeding* BALOO's *departure*). Well, I don't know where my mother's got to.

BALOO. Well, if you would mention about your Rory.

DEANNA. I'll tell her—don't you worry.

BALOO (*rising*). So, I'll say good night. (*She crosses to the door.*) I'll try and pop round again, because I would like to have had a word with Mrs. Hesseltine.

DEANNA (*discouragingly*). Well, you'll be lucky to catch her in.

BALOO. We can but try. (*Brightly.*) Good night!

DEANNA. Good night.

DESMOND. Good night, love.

(BALOO *goes out and the door closes behind her. We see her move past the yard, at the rear, as she goes down the street.*)

By bloody hell! She can yak, can't she? Yak-yak-yak! I thought she was going to be here all night. What's she supposed to be, anyway?

DEANNA. I don't know. She's the Baloo, isn't she?

DESMOND. I don't know. Don't ask me.

DEANNA. She is. She's the Baloo. She's, like, under the Cub Master.

(CHARLES *opens the door at the foot of the bedroom stairs and, after an apprehensive glance round the room, enters and crosses to his seat by the fire.*)

CHARLES. You want to stop letting people in. I've been sat up in that cold bedroom, when you've finished.

DEANNA. It's a pity for you.

CHARLES (*back in his old position*). Shur-rup and get out!

DEANNA. Get out yourself! It's not your house, is it? You've got a face like the back of a tram-smash when you're there!

CHARLES. Aw, shur-rup!

DESMOND (*still anxious to be off*). Anyway—

DEANNA. Are you going then, Desmond?

DESMOND. I'm not stopping here all night, am I?

(*There is a peremptory knock at the door and the door immediately opens.* OLD JAKIE *shuffles in with a newspaper in his hand, and stands by the door.*)

OLD JAKIE (*cheerfully*). I've lost it again!

DEANNA. Oh, you and that lavatory key. What would you do if we were out?

OLD JAKIE (*with a villainous laugh*). Have I to tell you?

(DEANNA *crosses and takes down the big lavatory key which hangs from a piece of string from a nail at the side of the door. She hands it to him and it drops from his fumbling fingers and falls on the floor.* OLD JAKIE *stoops, slowly, painfully and laboriously to pick it up.* DEANNA *continues to talk unconcernedly during* OLD JAKIE'S *exertions.*)

DEANNA. Go on then. And don't forget to lock it this time. And don't take it home with you, either.

(OLD JAKIE *finally retrieves the key and addresses* DESMOND *as he shuffles out.*)

OLD JAKIE. She's a bossy madam, isn't she?

(OLD JAKIE *goes out and the door closes behind him. During the following conversation we see* OLD JAKIE *cross into the yard and enter the third lavatory.*)

DEANNA. Honestly. He wants to wear that key round his neck. On a bit of string.

DESMOND. Are you coming out tomorrow night, then?

DEANNA. I don't know. Might do—might not.

DESMOND. We've started going up to Belle Isle estate, now. 'cause a lot of my mates have moved up there, now. And they've opened that new pub, you know. The Valley Arms. It's all right. It's all this modern.

DEANNA. What—you don't go right up there, do you?

DESMOND. 'course we do. Massive rooms, you know. You've got your concert-room, and you've got your singing-room with your piano as well. Beckett's house. You can sit outside if you want. It's all right. So are you coming, or not?

DEANNA. I'll see how I feel.

(DESMOND *crosses to the door.*)

DESMOND. Right. (*He opens the door and stands awkwardly, glancing at* CHARLES.) Right! (*Pause.*) Aren't you coming out for a minute, then?

DEANNA. I'm not going in that yard! Not while he's in. He stinks the place out, Old Jakie.

DESMOND. Well, if you won't, you won't. I'll get off then. So we'll leave it like that, eh? We'll expect you when we see you.

DEANNA. Yes. Goodnight.

DESMOND (*to them both*). Goodnight, then.

(CHARLES *does not reply.* DESMOND *goes out and we see him pass the yard on his way down the street. There is a silence as* DEANNA *moves around the room, picks up the cups and crosses to the sink, where she rinses them. Having rinsed the cups,* DEANNA *crosses and sits again on the shoe-box-cum stool by the fire. All the above has taken place in silence.*)

DEANNA. What did you go upstairs for, anyway? She'll think you're not right in the head.

CHARLES. It's you that's not right in your head. You want to stop telling people to come in—when you don't know them.

DEANNA. I do know her. You know her.

CHARLES. I don't know her.

DEANNA. She knows you, anyway.

CHARLES. Shut your gob.

(DEANNA *rises and crosses to the draining-board, where she pre- pares herself another slice of bread and dripping. We hear the sound of the flushing of the outside lavatory and* OLD JAKIE *shuffles out. He is still carrying the newspaper, which has now had a large section torn off. He locks the door and shuffles off, up the yard.* DEANNA *completes her spreading of the dripping and returns to her shoe-box as* OLD JAKIE, *after a peremptory knock at the door, enters.* OLD JAKIE *hangs the key on its nail.*)

JAKIE (*conversationally*). That's better.

DEANNA. Have you locked it?

JAKIE. I always lock it. It's not me that leaves it open, it's one of you.

DEANNA. It's not us, Jakie. Don't you put it on to us. It's you. 'cause I've proved it. 'cause last Sunday afternoon I thought, "Right, we'll just see." And I stood at that window waiting for you to go in.

And I went straight in after you and you'd left that door wide open.

JAKIE. I never went in last Sunday afternoon.

DEANNA. Don't come it with me. You don't know what you are doing half the time. You left that door wide open—there was every cat in Leopold Street sniffing round.

JAKIE. I never went down last Sunday afternoon.

DEANNA. Well, if you haven't locked it you'll know about it.

CHARLES (*without looking up*). Shur-rup about bloody closet door!

DEANNA. Shut up yourself, Misery!

JAKIE (*uninvited he shuffles across the room and ponderously seats himself on the sofa*). He's working then, is he, your dad?

DEANNA. Yes. He's down at the Builders Arms with my mam.

JAKIE. Where's your Harry then? Is he down there as well?

DEANNA. No, he works late now. Eleven o'clock last night. He's left Dixon's Boilers, didn't you know? He left on Tuesday. He hit a fellow. He's driving now. He works for—oh, what they call them? Them big green vans. Fisher's Haulage. He reckons he'll be going all over. Delivering. You've seen his van outside here at night, haven't you? He brought it home last night.

JAKIE. I looked out of my window last night—I saw that van. Well, I thought, there's nobody in this street has a van.

DEANNA (*with pride*). That's his van. Our Harry's. They let him fetch it home. Well, they don't know he's fetching it home, but if he's working late it doesn't matter. They don't care.

JAKIE. Does he have it at weekends?

DEANNA. I don't know. He might be able to swing it, though. Why?

JAKIE. Well, you know that crippled woman that used to live down Rufus Street? Her that's gone up to the new estate. Well, she's got a chest of drawers she says I can have. If I can get anybody to fetch it.

DEANNA. He might fetch it for you. Give him a couple of bob.

> (ALBERT *and* QUEENIE HESSELTINE *come down the street and we see them pass the top of the yard.*)

JAKIE. Couple of bob? I haven't got any couple of bobs to give away. I haven't got a couple of bob for myself. He'll do it for me.

> (*The door opens and* ALBERT *and* QUEENIE *enter. They have both been drinking rather heavily, but are too experienced drinkers for it to have any outward effect—apart from emphasizing their natural garrulousness.*)

QUEENIE (*taking up an argument with* ALBERT *that has been going on since they left the Builders Arms*). So if you think I'm sitting there all night like Dopey Alice you've got another think coming. I was sitting there from ten past nine—by their clock—ten past nine till quarter to ten, and I never had a drink. Herbert came in twice to take my glass away—he thought I'd finished.

ALBERT. Shut your row! You're lucky to get anything! You'll stop at home next time!

QUEENIE. I'll go out on my own, never mind stop at home.

ALBERT. You'll go on your own! It's cheaper for me! You go on your own! Suit your bloody self!

QUEENIE (*taking off her coat*). Don't you come that. Don't you come that with me. You give me the money. You just give me the money.

ALBERT. I'll give you a kick up the backside, never mind money.

QUEENIE. Get away with you, you stingy cow—you are one. (*Turning to* DEANNA *for support.*) Do you know what he's bought me all night? Do you know what he's had the cheek to send me in? Two Double Diamonds! (*She lifts up two fingers in emphasis.*)   Two! Two! That's all he's sent me in—all night.

DEANNA. You've had more than two.

QUEENIE. I have had more than two. But that stingy cow didn't buy them. (*Turning again to* ALBERT.) You stingy cow!

ALBERT. I don't know why you sit in that room. I haven't time to go running in there. Why don't you sit in the Best Room, same as everybody else?

QUEENIE (*indicating the old pinafore which she is wearing*). How can I sit in the Best Room in this?

ALBERT. You keep your coat on, you gormless bitch! (*Turning to* JAKIE *for support.*) By bloody hell! She hasn't the sense she was born with!

QUEENIE. If I don't slit your throat one of these days. (*She crosses to the sideboard taking a packet of crisps from her pocket.*) And don't you go touching these crisps, our Charles! They're our Rory's, is these.

CHARLES (*without glancing up*). Shur-rup about crisps. You're always on about crisps.

DEANNA. Hey! Hey, mam! You know our Rory's not been going to the Cubs, don't you?

QUEENIE (*swinging round*). You what! He'd better have been going to the Cubs. After I've bought him that uniform.

DEANNA. Well, he hasn't then. 'cause that Baloo's been round. They've not clapped eyes on him for three weeks.

QUEENIE (*keenly interested*). You what?

DEANNA. He's been taking his money and floating off somewhere. (*Counting off on her fingers.*) He wasn't there tonight, he wasn't there last week and he wasn't there the week before. So that's ninepence he owes you—subs.

QUEENIE (*with mounting anger*). He's had more than flaming ninepence!

I've been giving him twopence a week besides, for his camp. And what did he ask for last week? Another threepence for the Flag Day! (*She suddenly bursts into action, moving towards the bedroom stairs.*) I'll murder that kid! I'll mark him for life, I will! (*She disappears up the bedroom stairs still shouting.*) Rory. Rory! What have you been doing with that money! And why haven't you been going to them Cubs?

> (ALBERT, CHARLES, DEANNA *and* OLD JAKIE *remain completely still and silent, respectfully and expectantly waiting for the first blow.* OLD JAKIE *breaks the silence.*)

JAKIE (*gleefully*). He'll cop it!

> (*Another pause and then, suddenly, hell is let loose in the bedroom.* JAKIE *speaks with self-satisfaction.*)

He's copping it!

QUEENIE (*we hear her voice indistinctly*). Get up! Get up, you little midden! Get up! What have you been doing with that money? Where's that ninepence? Eh? Eh? Where is it? Where's that money?

RORY (*off*). Ommi! Ommi! My sore arm!

QUEENIE (*off*). I'll sore arm you! And where've you been going every Friday night?

RORY (*off*). Geroff. Geroff. My sore arm!

QUEENIE (*off*). Why haven't you been going to them Cubs? Where's that money?

> (*The noise in the bedroom subsides slightly into an indeterminate mixture of blows, abuse and screams. The occupants of the living-room relax and the conversation continues.*)

JAKIE (*tolerantly to* ALBERT). She's a devil when she gets started, isn't she? Your Queenie?

ALBERT (*with pride*). She bashes him. She belts him. Do you know, she can go at him for half an hour. It's like water off a duck's back. She'll kill him one of these days. (*Dismissing the subject he crosses to the table and begins to unload about six shillings' worth of pennies and halfpennies from his jacket pocket.*) It's a ton weight, this lot.

JAKIE (*in admiration*). How much have you got there, then?

ALBERT. I haven't had a chance to count it. Six bob—seven bob. He won't miss it.

JAKIE. Well, what do you do then? Do you short-change them?

ALBERT. I don't. I don't short-change my mates. No, I give him short—the landlord—when I reckon up. He doesn't notice. He never misses it—he's rolling in it. It's coming out of his ears.

DEANNA. You'll get caught one of these days.

ALBERT. Get away with you. Anyway, he's got more than I have. (*He picks up about a shillingsworth of coppers and gives them to* JAKIE.) Here. Don't say I never give you nothing.

JAKIE (*examining it*). What's this for?

ALBERT. Don't you want it? I can spend it if you can't. It's for that cauliflower you got for me—off Jackie Tattersall.

JAKIE (*pocketing the money*). It'll come in, will that.

ALBERT. And you found it, if anybody wants to know.

JAKIE. I don't say anything. I never say nothing.

(*At which point* QUEENIE *comes down the stairs, still hurling abuse at the bedroom.* RORY'S *screams have now dissolved into a monotonous weeping which can be heard downstairs.*)

QUEENIE (*off*). And you stop in all next week! And you don't go to no pictures or nowhere else! (*She appears at the bottom of the stairs and, holding the door open, screams again.*) I'm going to burn that Cub uniform tomorrow morning! And are you going to stop that crying? Or have I to come up there and give you something to cry for? (*The crying stops abruptly.* QUEENIE *bangs the door shut.*) I'll mark him for life one of these days, I will! I'll cut his hands off if he doesn't stop taking things!

ALBERT. Had he got that bedroom light on?

QUEENIE. He hadn't got that bedroom light on—'cause he knows what he'd get if he had.

JAKIE. He's a lad and a half, that one.

ALBERT. You don't know. What he is. (*To* QUEENIE.) And tell him to stop that bloody singing every night, or I will. Then he'll know about it. (*To* JAKIE.) He does. He sits up singing in bed. Haven't you heard him in your house? You can hear him halfway down our street.

QUEENIE. He's got too much off for nine years old.

JAKIE. He's a lad and a half, that one.

QUEENIE (*crossing and taking up the bag of crisps*). Well, he doesn't get these tomorrow now. He can wait for them. (*She crosses and places the crisps on the shelf above the sink.*) The little flamer.

JAKIE (*laboriously rising to his feet*). Well, I'll be in for my chips tomorrow. (*He shuffles slowly towards the door.*)

ALBERT. You'll get no chips. Why don't you buy your own bloody chips?

JAKIE. I've got no money for chips. (*He pauses at the door and indicates the copper on the table.*) You want to get that put away.

ALBERT. Go on! Get out of it!

(OLD JAKIE *shuffles out, leaving the door partly open.* ALBERT *calls out after him.*)

Door!

QUEENIE (*crossing and slamming the door*). He was born in a flaming field, that one!

DEANNA. You want to tell him about that lavvy door, as well. He always leaves that wide open.

QUEENIE (*shivering elaborately*). Oooh, it's like winter! (*She glances at the fireplace.*) Who's let that fire go out? (*To* CHARLES.) Have you? Have you sat there and watched it go out?

(QUEENIE *crosses and begins to poke the fire enthusiastically.* CHARLES *shows signs of exasperation.*)

CHARLES. Give over! You can't leave it alone five minutes.

(QUEENIE *makes a great show of attempting to revive the fire. She pulls out the grate, puts on coal with her hands and generally disturbs* CHARLES, *who gathers up his papers in annoyance.*)

QUEENIE. Don't move, will you!

(CHARLES, *letting out an elaborate sigh of exasperation, takes his books and papers and moves to the sofa, where he immediately settles down again.*)

I'll be glad to see the last of this house. I will. It's every night alike. I'll be glad when they do pull them down. These houses. If they don't fall down. (*She turns viciously to* ALBERT *and her voice rises and takes on an almost hysterical tone.*) He won't do that window! He says he won't do it! He says it's the tenant—sash-cords.

ALBERT. Is it bloody hellers like the tenant. Who told you that tale?

QUEENIE. Rent man.

ALBERT. You take no notice of the rent man. Did you pay him?

QUEENIE. Well, we had to pay something off.

ALBERT (*furious*). What did you want to pay him for? What have I told you? You don't pay no bloody rent—and you don't pay no bloody arrears—he gets nothing! Until he does them jobs. (*He lists them on his fingers.*) There's your sash-cords to do. There's your fireback. (*Going off into a fresh fury at the thought.*) You won't get no fire there, you know. You can kneel there all night. You can see the bloody street through that crack! There's your cellar steps—I'll break my back on them one of these days. There's your slates. And I'm not putting that floorboard in upstairs.

DEANNA (*reasoning*). Well, you took it out.

ALBERT. I don't care who took it out—I'm not putting it back. They can whistle for it.

QUEENIE. Well, you know the Council won't give you a house until you've got a clean rent-book.

ALBERT. We'll never get a council house. Can you see us in a council house? We've been getting a council house for ten years.

DEANNA. You don't know. They're pulling them all down—all round St. Christopher's.

ALBERT (*his anger abating*). Any road, he can mend that fireback before they pull this down.

> (ALBERT *crosses and sits by the table, stacking the coppers into piles. There is a brief silence which is broken by the voice of* RORY *singing in a cracked treble.*)

RORY (*off*). "A frog he would a wooing go,
Heigh-ho says Roly.
Whether his mother would let him or no,
With a Roly-poly, gammon and spinach,
Heigh-ho says Anthony Roly—"

> (*Before* RORY *has completed his song* QUEENIE, *her temper again rising, has slammed down the poker and marched to the foot of the stairs.*)

QUEENIE (*screaming*). Will you stop that row! If I've to tell you once more! Do you hear me! (*The singing ends abruptly.*)

> (QUEENIE *crosses back into the room and over to the fireplace. She glances despairingly at the fire, which has defeated her efforts.*)

Oh well, bubbles to it. It can go out. You can all freeze for all I care.

DEANNA. Isn't there any supper?

ALBERT. Supper? What do you want supper for? We're going to bed—never mind bloody supper.

DEANNA. It's all right for you. You had a big tea. I've only had a plateful of chips and some bread and dripping, that's all.

QUEENIE. Whose fault is that? Silly cat. You go gadding out—straight from work and then you come home and say you're hungry! I'm not here to wait on you, you know.

DEANNA. Well, you could have brought some fish and chips in, couldn't you? It wouldn't have broken your arm, carrying them.

QUEENIE. I'm not queueing up for you, or nobody else. You can get your own fish and chips.

ALBERT. There's too many fish and chips eaten in this house. You want to start cooking. If I'm not fed up of flaming bacon. It's every night alike. Bacon, bacon.

QUEENIE. Well, we've got it to eat, we can't let it go to waste. Our Harry went to a lot of trouble getting that.

ALBERT. He'll finish up in the nick, he will. Did you give Old Jakie any?

QUEENIE. Well, I gave him a piece.

ALBERT. I hope you told him to keep his mouth shut. 'cause you know what he's like. He'd have it on the nine-o'clock news, he would.

QUEENIE. He's all right.

ALBERT (*rising*). Anyway, I'm not stopping up. There's no bloody fire, there's nothing to bloody eat. I'm off to bed, that's where I'm off.

DEANNA. There's some bread and dripping, if you want some.

ALBERT. I don't want no bread and dripping.

DEANNA. It's pork dripping, you know. It's not beef dripping.

ALBERT (*not wishing to argue*). It needs to be. (*He makes a move towards the bedroom stairs as we hear the sound of a van approaching up the street.*)

QUEENIE (*glancing at the clock on the mantelpiece*). That's our Harry. I suppose he'll want something now.

> (*We hear the van pull up outside the house and we see the headlights across the yard. The headlights are switched off.*)

ALBERT. Give him bacon, then. Give him a bacon sandwich, let's get shut of it. (*With interest.*) Where's he been today, then?

DEANNA. Stradhoughton.

> (*The door opens and* HARRY LAUDER HESSELTINE *enters. He is carrying a cardboard carton under his arm.*)

HARRY. Now then! Did you fetch us a bottle back, our old lad?

ALBERT. Did I hellers like. (*Indicating the carton.*) What the hell have you come home with this time?

> (HARRY *crosses and tips the contents of the carton on the table. About twenty-five small packets of liquorice allsorts spill out on to the table.* ALBERT *puts his hand out to protect the small piles of copper.*)

Mind my change!

QUEENIE (*crossing to examine the sweets*). What the hamlet have you got now? You'll get us all shot.

HARRY. What's up with you? It's only liquorice allsorts.

DEANNA. Where do you get these from? (*She picks up a packet and opens it.*) They're all right, aren't they?

HARRY. I won them.

ALBERT. Yes, I've seen you win things before. I've told you, you don't come running to me for bail money.

HARRY (*as* DEANNA *starts to eat the contents of the packet*). Who said you could have one?

QUEENIE (*taking charge of the proceedings*). She can have that and we're putting these away. They'll come in, will these. And don't tell our Rory where I've put them—'cause he's only having one. (*She starts putting the packets back in the carton.*)

HARRY (*turning to* CHARLES). Get your shoes on, our kid.

CHARLES. What's up?

HARRY. Come on. (*Moving towards the door.*) I want a strong pair of hands.

> (CHARLES *fishes his shoes from under the sofa and slips them on.*)

ALBERT (*suspiciously*). Why? What you got now?

HARRY (*proudly*). You wait! Just wait there! You've never seen nothing like this! Come on, our kid!

CHARLES (*crossing reluctantly to the door*). You can't sit down for five minutes in this house.

(HARRY *and* CHARLES *go out, leaving the door open. The others wait expectantly. After a few moments' pause* HARRY *and* CHARLES *stagger in bearing between them a carved wooden lectern surmounted by an elaborate eagle.*)

ALBERT. What in God's name have you got now!

(HARRY *and* CHARLES *stand the lectern in front of the fireplace.*)

DEANNA. What is it?

HARRY. I don't know. It's all right though, isn't it? (*He points proudly to the eagle.*) There's some work there, you know. It's all hand done.

DEANNA. Where did you get it from?

QUEENIE. Never mind where you got it from, it goes straight back, does that. It's too much of a good thing, is this.

HARRY. I found it. (ALBERT *gives him a long sceptical look.*) I did! I found it! (*To* CHARLES.) You know that car park where you used to work? Well, you know that piece of waste ground that goes down just by the side of it. Well, it was there. I'm driving along and I see this thing in my headlights. I thought it was a big bloody bird.

DEANNA. Well, it is a bird, isn't it?

HARRY. No, you daft bitch! I mean a real one. So I gets out and has a look. And there it is. I'd hell's own job getting it in the van, I can tell you. Somebody must have thrown it away.

ALBERT. Nobody's going to throw a thing like that away.

CHARLES. Well, what's it supposed to be, when it's there?

HARRY. I don't know. I bet it's worth a lot of money, though.

ALBERT (*who has been scrutinizing the lectern*). It's German is that. (*Indicating the eagle.*) You know what that is, don't you? That's your German eagle. You see it all over in Germany. Deutschland Uber Allies. I've come across scores of them in the army.

QUEENIE (*her anger mounting*). I don't care whether it's German or French or German or what it is. It goes out. It's getting beyond a joke is this. You can stop fetching stuff home.

HARRY. What's up with you?

QUEENIE. Never mind what's up or what's down. We're not having that in this house. So be told.

HARRY. I found it! You're all right, what you worrying about?

QUEENIE. Never mind whether you found it or you didn't find it, it goes back. It goes back where you got it from. It's not a dumping-ground, isn't this. There's our Charles has had a sack of staples down there in the cellar for I don't know how long! I don't know what he fetched them for. (*Indicating* ALBERT.) There's him with his bottles piled on top of the wardrobe. (*Speaking directly to* ALBERT.) You brought them in, you can take them out again. (*To* HARRY.)

And there's you with your German eagles. If I'm not sick of the lot of you! Well, it's not stopping in this house!

HARRY (*jocularly trying to placate her*). It's all right. It'll go in your bedroom.

QUEENIE. It goes in nobody's bedroom! It goes straight back!

(HARRY, *with heavily simulated patience, looks up at the ceiling. There is a silence and, once again, we hear the clear cracked tones of* RORY *singing in bed.*)

RORY (*off*). "All things bright and beautiful
All creatures great and small.
All things wise and wonderful,
The Lord God made them all."

(QUEENIE, *who is now in a complete fury, grabs the nearest weapon at hand which is a high-heeled shoe on the sofa. Without a word she charges up the stairs.* DEANNA, ALBERT, CHARLES *and* HARRY, *ignoring this diversion, gather round the lectern admiringly.* RORY, *unaware that his mother is approaching, continues his song.*)

(*off.*) "The rich man in his castle,
The poor man at the gate.
He made them high and lowly,
Each to his own estate. . . ."

CURTAIN

ACT TWO

The following morning—Saturday.

When the curtain rises, the living-room and yard are deserted. There is a pause of some moments before QUEENIE *marches down the bedroom stairs and into the living-room.* QUEENIE *is bearing in her hands a complete Wolf Cub uniform surmounted by the green and gold cap. Without pausing she crosses to the door, goes out and, a moment later, enters the yard.* QUEENIE *crosses to the lower dustbin, lifts the lid with a flourish and dumps the uniform in the bin with an air of finality. She slams the lid down and returns into the house.* QUEENIE *crosses to the table, which is strewn with the debris of breakfast—milk bottle, corn-flake packet, jam jar, sliced loaf still in its wrapping, etc. She is pouring herself a cup of tea as* CHARLES *pads down the bedroom stairs and enters the living-room.* CHARLES *is in his stockinged feet, shirtsleeves and braces. He is carrying his form-books which, in fact, go with him everywhere about the house. He crosses to his usual chair by the fire without acknowledging* QUEENIE'S *presence.*

QUEENIE (*speaking conversationally*). You'll get no breakfast—sitting over there. (CHARLES *makes no reply.*) I'm fed up of all crumbs and crusts all over the show. If I've swept up once this morning I've swept up ten times.

CHARLES. What is it? Bacon?

QUEENIE. No, it isn't bacon. If you want bacon you can get up like everybody else. There's corn flakes, there's sugar puffs, and there's a slice of fried bread in the oven. So you can get on with it.

(CHARLES, *without replying, reaches over and takes the plate containing the fried bread from the old-fashioned oven, used only for this purpose, by the fire.* QUEENIE, *at the table, pours* CHARLES *a mug of tea.*)

CHARLES (*examining the fried bread he speaks with great indignation*). Is this all there is? It's all dried up, is this.

QUEENIE. Get it down you. Stop moaning. (*She hands him the mug of tea.*) Here.

CHARLES. How long's this been made?

QUEENIE. Get it drunk! It's only been made half an hour. I made it fresh for our Rory. And then he didn't drink it. He's skipped off. He thinks I don't know where he's gone—but I do. He's gone to that Saturday picture-house club. That's where he's gone. Well, just wait till he gets home. I'll picture-house club him, I will. He'll be black and blue by the time I've finished. (*She speaks conversationally.*) I'll kill him. He won't be going to no Saturday picture-house club next week—'cause he'll be six feet under by the time I've finished with him. He will. He'll be pushing up daisies.

CHARLES (*chewing and reading*). Shur-rup about bloody Saturday picture club!

QUEENIE (*ignoring* CHARLES). He knew very well what he had to do for me this morning. That's why he went waltzing off. There's his errands to do, for one. (*Raising her voice shrilly.*) I'm not going to that Co-op! He's still going—he doesn't get out of it! If he comes in at midnight he's still going! (*Resuming her natural voice.*) There's the cobbler's to go to. His father's shoes to fetch. And he wants them for tonight, so there's no getting out of that one. And I promised to lend him to Old Jakie for half an hour this morning. 'cause he wants him to take that old pram and fetch a bag of coke that he's getting from a chap, down Isle End Road.

CHARLES. Shur-rup about Rory! (*He pauses.*) Anyway, I thought he was supposed to be getting that there for me this morning.

QUEENIE. What?

CHARLES (*impatiently*). That paint, dozy!

QUEENIE. What paint?

CHARLES. That paint! What's up with you? What I'm getting off that bloke.

QUEENIE (*recollecting*). Oh, yes! We know all about that. You and your paint. What did I tell you about that paint? I told you if you want that paint you go down and fetch it yourself. You don't send our Rory. He's too young for that. 'cause you know what it is, don't you? It's receiving. It's a very serious crime, if you did but know it. Receiving. It's all right for you, if you get caught—you can talk your way out of it. But our little Rory can't. He'll just stand there like an whore at a wedding. He'll blab the whole lot out. He's not old enough.

CHARLES (*dismissing her in his usual manner*). Shur-rup!

QUEENIE (*rising and making desultory effort to clear the table*). It's all right you talking. It's me that'll drop in for it in the finish. You don't seem to understand. (*With emphasis.*) It's receiving! And it's always the householder where the goods is that cops in for it. Well, it's me that's the householder—not him. It's my name that's on the rent-book. It's not his name, it's my name. If I drop dead tomorrow you'll all be out in the street. Camping out. It's me that's liable. You see there's that big wooden bird that our Harry's fetched home. Well, he says he's found it, but it's just the same—stealing by finding. I'll be glad when we've got shut of it. (*Her voice rising again.*) What's he want to bring it home for anyway? What good is it? It's neither use nor ornament.

CHARLES. It's all this carving—what's up with you?

QUEENIE. Well, it's old! It's all old-fashioned! They don't have that nowadays. I mean, your Jacobean sideboards, they've gone out. You don't see them now. It's all matt finish these days.

CHARLES. Anyway, whose lavatory are we supposed to be using?

QUEENIE. Well, that's the trouble! That's what I'm saying. We can't be doing with it stuck in there! You can't be running up and down Leopold Street borrowing everybody's keys. I've been using Mallinson's this morning. Well, of course, she wants to know what's going on. Well, I don't know what to tell her.

CHARLES. Tell her to mind her own business.

QUEENIE. How can you? When people's doing you favours? I had to make up a tale. I had to tell her that your father's gone off with our key in his pocket.

CHARLES (*rhetorically*). Isn't there any more fried bread?

QUEENIE. No, there isn't any more fried bread. (*Reverting to her train of thought.*) I'll be glad when we've got an inside toilet. The sooner we get out of these houses the better. The sooner they pull them all down and get us into them council houses, I'll breathe a sigh of relief. That's what I'll do. I will. I'll breathe a sigh of relief. And there'll be no putting stuff in the toilet then, I'll tell you that. And there'll be no fetching stuff home then—none of you. 'cause you don't know who you might be living next to, on these new estates. (*She glances round at her meagre possessions.*) And we're going to have a bonfire in this street before we go. We're going to burn the lot. All this furniture can go. All of it. 'cause I'm sick of seeing it. We're going to have all new. We're going to have a kitchen table—Formica top. And you eat your meals in the kitchen and nowhere else. And we're going to have a proper carpet. And we're going to have a matt finish sideboard—all modern. And there'll be no toys kept in it. And the first scratch on that sideboard, there'll be murder done in that house. (*We see* BALOO *cross the end of the yard.*) And you can all be thinking about gardening as well, before we get there. 'cause it's got to be done—else they chuck you out.

(*There is a knock at the door.* QUEENIE, *who is crossing to the sink with her hands full of cups and pots, turns and addresses* CHARLES.) Don't answer it, will you? (*She places the crockery in the sink and crosses towards the door.*) You might break your leg if you get up. (*She opens the door, but continues to berate* CHARLES *without even looking who the caller is.*) Well, don't think I'm having you sitting there on your backside all morning, 'cause you're not. 'cause I'm fed up of seeing you there with your racing-books and tips and I don't know what else. (*Hysteria again creeps into her voice.*) You never win nothing! They get it all back even when you do win! (*She turns and looks coldly at* BALOO.)

BALOO. Good morning. Mrs. Hesseltine?

QUEENIE. Yes . . .?

BALOO. Could I come in for a minute? I'm Baloo—from the Cubs.

>   (QUEENIE *walks into the room, allowing* BALOO *to follow her.*
> BALOO *is dressed in her everyday clothes. She wears a cheap two-piece suit and carries a shapeless handbag. Her clothes are sensible without being frumpish.* CHARLES, *seeing* BALOO, *immediately rises and, carrying his books and papers, retreats upstairs to his bedroom.* QUEENIE, *although annoyed at* RORY, *is indignant towards* BALOO *because of her previous night's tale-telling to* DEANNA. QUEENIE, *where strangers are concerned, possesses a strong primitive and natural mothering instinct towards her young.*)

QUEENIE. I've heard all about it, thank you very much. So you can't tell me anything I don't know already. Anyway, he's not the only one. There's plenty more skips the Cubs besides him.

BALOO. Not as many as you might think, Mrs. Hesseltine. Actually it's quite encouraging. Once we get them there and they see what activities there are available, they do tend to stay with us.

QUEENIE. Well, he doesn't. He's finished with them. He's chucked out. 'cause I've chucked him out. I've chucked his uniform out. And I shall chuck him out as well, when he walks through that door. I'll chuck him out through the window.

BALOO. I don't know whether it's been explained to you—that it's not entirely his fault.

QUEENIE. I know whose fault it is. It's them Cubs. All of them that belongs. He's got like them.

BALOO (*attempting to interrupt*). Oh, I think that—

QUEENIE (*refusing to listen*). Oh, I know you think different. You don't see them like we do. They're all right while they're in that Scout Hut. It's when they get outside. Running up and down this street. Calling after people. Shouting and swearing. They pinch milk—I've seen a lad pinching milk—he was one of yours.

BALOO (*again attempting to interrupt*). Oh, I think you must be—

QUEENIE (*sailing on*). He did! He took a pint bottle from that little woman at the top of our street. (BALOO *sits.*) Then he didn't drink it. He took one swig and he smashed it against that lamp-post. 'cause I watched him do it. I said, "You destructive little swine!" He comes out with a right mouthful. That's where our Rory gets it from. He was never like that. But he is now. He's a little demon. He's a devil! He's a little cow. He's a right little cow, that's what he is, these days.

BALOO. Well, if that was one of our boys I've got a very shrewd suspicion who it might be.

QUEENIE. I can tell you who it was, love. He always wears wellingtons and he's got two yellow stripes round his arm.

BALOO. Michael Shepherd. He's a sixer. Well, he won't have two yellow stripes on Friday, I can assure you. You see, we do have our black sheep.

QUEENIE (cutting in). I'll yellow stripe him, I will.

BALOO. In fact, I'll go so far as to say he'll be most fortunate if he isn't divested from the pack.

QUEENIE. It was a full pint he threw!

BALOO. Michael is definitely the ringleader, he needs a stronger influence than we can give him.

QUEENIE. He wants locking up, that one.

BALOO. He's beyond our control—he's beyond parental control. At least Rory does have parents who are interested in his movements.

QUEENIE. Don't ask me about his movements, missis. I don't know where he gets to. I don't know where he is now.

BALOO. Well, what we are hoping is that you'll be able to tell us where he was last night.

QUEENIE. We know where he wasn't, don't we? He had his threepence, he went off as large as life. Anyway, it's in the dustbin—all of it: cap, garter-tabs, neckerchief, woggle, jersey—the lot. He's had it.

BALOO. I'm afraid it's more serious than that. He may have to account for where he was at seven-fifteen last night.

(QUEENIE, *realizing by long-practised instinct that there is trouble, is immediately on the defensive.*)

QUEENIE. How do you mean?

(BALOO *rises, crosses to the table and peels off her gloves. She stands rather like a prosecutrix, and as she speaks assembles notes from her handbag.* QUEENIE *leans across the table and listens keenly for some specific accusation against* RORY *which she can immediately refute.*)

BALOO. Early yesterday evening it was discovered that St. Christopher's Church had been broken into again. There's been repeated desecration there ever since the church was closed. There have been obscenities chalked up and some filthy, obscene beast has urinated against the wall. But the main feature of last night's vandalism is that the lectern has been wrenched up and taken away.

QUEENIE. You what?

BALOO. The lectern. A beautiful piece of work. (BALOO *again flutters out her hands in demonstration.*) A beautifully carved eagle. The work of a craftsman.

QUEENIE (*not actively on the defensive*). Just a minute, missis. We want witnesses for this. (*She crosses to the bedroom stairs and calls up in irritation.*) D'you hear me!

CHARLES (*off, and also in irritation*). What?

QUEENIE. Would you mind just stepping downstairs for a minute.

> (QUEENIE *crosses and sits by the table stolidly.* BALOO *attempts to speak.*)

BALOO. Now, I'm not making any specific—

QUEENIE (*interrupting*). Just a minute, missis. Just hold your horses.

> (*There is a silence as they wait for* CHARLES *to appear.* QUEENIE *remains impassive, while* BALOO *is rather embarrassed.* CHARLES *enters.*)

CHARLES (*gruffly*). What's up?

> (QUEENIE, *now that her witness is here, ignores* CHARLES *completely and turns to* BALOO.)

QUEENIE. Now then. You just go on saying what you were saying about our Rory.

BALOO (*realizing that she is on dangerous ground, speaks carefully*). We're not making any specific allegations, Mrs. Hesseltine. It's just that there is some evidence—

QUEENIE (*again interrupting*). You just want to be careful with your accusals—who you go round accusing. (*As* QUEENIE *continues* BALOO *tries to get a word in, but fails as* QUEENIE *flattens her with a sheer weight of words.*) 'cause he's not like that, isn't our Rory. He doesn't take things—'cause he knows what he'll get if he did. (*She reflects for a moment and then corrects herself in the light of facts known to* BALOO.) He might take threepence or fourpence, but he wouldn't take big things.

BALOO. It's not a question of theft, it's a question of vandalism. Possibly even a childhood prank.

QUEENIE (*addressing* CHARLES, *speaks over* BALOO's *last words—it is not so much an interruption but rather an ignoring of* BALOO's *argument*). This lady's come here with an accusal. (*Meaningly.*) She reckons our Rory has broken into that old church and taken a big wooden bird.

BALOO. A lectern.

QUEENIE (*still ignoring* BALOO). Now you just tell this lady where our Rory was at a quarter past seven last night. Seven-fifteen.

CHARLES (*the alibi coming naturally to him*). He was with me—where do you think he was?

QUEENIE (*quickly and encouragingly*). Yes, well, tell the lady where he was and what he was doing. She knows he wasn't at the Cubs.

(*As* CHARLES *speaks* QUEENIE *turns to* BALOO, *giving her an expansive smile in which there is some maternal pride in* CHARLES'S *accomplishments as a liar.*)

CHARLES (*in a courtroom monotone*). Half past six to half past seven: in here. Reading a comic. Half past seven–eight o'clock: fish shop. 'cause I sent him and I stood at that door and watched him all the way down the street. And he was never out of my sight—so that clears that. Comes home, watches telly, goes to bed. (*He pauses to see how* BALOO *is taking this and then offers her corroborative evidence.*) It was a fish and threepennorth he fetched for me.

BALOO (*unhappily*). Well, apparently he was seen with three other Cubs. You see, Mr. Sissons, the caretaker, is quite sure that he saw him. He names your Rory and Michael Shepherd.

QUEENIE. Well, you tell Mr. Sissons from me that he needs his eyes testing. 'cause we've got a witness. (*To* CHARLES.) 'cause Old Jakie saw him as well, didn't he?

CHARLES. Jakie'll speak up for him.

QUEENIE (*with finality*). So you'd better take your accusals somewhere else, missis.

(BALOO *is about to speak, but then, realizing that she is fighting a losing battle, she draws on her gloves, picks up her handbag and moves towards the door.*)

BALOO. I'm afraid you're taking a very shortsighted view of things, Mrs. Hesseltine.

(QUEENIE, *emboldened by* BALOO'S *retreat, waves her hand offensively.*)

QUEENIE. Go on. Get off! Get on with you!

BALOO (*pausing at the door*). Because I shall have to make my report to the Vicar.

QUEENIE (*genial in her victory*). Make it to who you like, love. Make it to King Kong, if you like. You can go see the Vicar. (*In a gust of anger.*) Because I shall go and see that bloody Vicar myself. You're all alike. You send him home from Sunday school with his little palm cross in his hand and the next minute you're threatening Borstal. You call yourself churchgoers—

(BALOO, *again about to speak, again changes her mind and abruptly marches out of the house.* CHARLES *crosses and takes up his accustomed position by the fire.* QUEENIE *stands smouldering with anger for some moments; but when she speaks we find that now that the immediate emergency is past her anger is directed against* RORY.)

The stupid little swine. Just wait till he gets in. I'll take the poker to him, I will. (*Directly to* CHARLES.) You'll have to stop me—because if I start on him I'll kill him.

CHARLES. What's up with you? He didn't bring it home. It was our Harry that fetched it in.

QUEENIE. Never mind who fetched it in. Our Harry found it. He didn't go breaking into churches, dragging it through the streets in broad daylight. The daft, dozy little devil!

CHARLES. Shur-rup!

QUEENIE. I'm sick of that kid. I am. I'm sick of you. I'm sick of all of you. I'd leave here tomorrow. I'd leave the lot of you. If I could get into that new house on my own and leave you lot behind I'd be off tomorrow. Bags packed. Because you're nothing but trouble. There's our Rory treading muck in and fingermarking the walls. There's our Harry trailing wooden birds in and I don't know what else. There's him drunk every night. There's her, mucky underclothes all over the house. There's you, cluttering up the place with your books and papers. Why don't you get some shoes on for a change? And you all tread crumbs all over the place. Why can't you sit at the table? I could have that house looking beautiful. I could have a beautiful house—if you'd let me. A lovely home. Only you'll spoil everything.

(*There is a silence as* QUEENIE *is lost in her dreams of Utopia.* CHARLES *continues to stare moodily into the fire. The silence is broken by the sound of* HARRY'S *van approaching along the street and pulling up outside the house.* QUEENIE, *without moving, speaks without raising her voice.*)

There's them two middens here now.

(*The front door opens and* ALBERT *and* HARRY *enter. They are dressed in what is for them "casual-style", i.e. untorn jacket over working clothes. They are both angry, but their anger is smouldering underneath rather than on the surface.* ALBERT *nods towards* CHARLES *and speaks to no one in particular.*)

ALBERT. Well, he can get his coat on, 'cause they'll be round for him in a minute. They'll be round for us all.

CHARLES (*glancing up*). What's up with you?

ALBERT (*to* QUEENIE). You as well. We'll all be inside by four o'clock this afternoon.

QUEENIE (*bursting with her own news*). There's somebody will be inside—our Rory. He'll be in that reform school.

ALBERT. Never mind about Rory. We've got more than him on us plates. Do you know what that silly old swine's been doing? Old Jakie? He's only been going all round Top Moor Side blabbing his mouth off about that wooden bird.

QUEENIE (*flopping on a chair in defeat*). Oh my God. I knew. I knew the minute that bird came into the house there'd be trouble. Why couldn't you all leave it alone? Why do you always have to be taking things and taking things?

HARRY (*beginning the story*). We goes up to the new estate to pick up that chest of drawers. (*A sudden gust of anger.*) It was for him we were doing it! We were doing him a favour! (*The anger drops as he returns to the story.*) Woman comes to the door. She says, "Oh, I hear Old Jakie can't get into the toilet." He's only told her what's in there. He's told her. He's told Sidney Jeffries. He's told Harry Chandler. I don't know who he hasn't told.

ALBERT (*resentfully*). He should be dead and buried at his age anyway.

QUEENIE (*although worried she is proud at the extra titbit of information she holds*). Right. I'll tell you something now. Do you know where that bird comes from?

HARRY. 'course I know where it came from. Came from that waste ground.

ALBERT (*to* HARRY). What's it matter where it came from? It's German. It's a German eagle.

(QUEENIE *has waited with exaggerated patience for this exchange to finish.*)

QUEENIE (*politely*). Have you finished? Have you quite finished? Because if you're sure you're quite finished I'll just tell you where that bird came from. That bird came from St. Christopher's Church. It's what they put the Holy Bible on.

HARRY (*realizing the fact.*) Oooh hell.

ALBERT (*resignedly*). We'll get fifteen years. We'll get fifteen years apiece. Blasphemy that comes under.

(QUEENIE, *pleased with the effect of her words, has again been waiting for the exchange to end before dropping her final bombshell.*)

QUEENIE. Now then. How did the bird get on to the waste ground from the church? (*Pausing for effect.*) Well, I'll tell you. Someone took it there, didn't they? (*Again pausing.*) Who took it there? Well, I'll tell you that as well. (*To* ALBERT.) A certain little lad— they call him Rory..

ALBERT (*quietly*). Bloody hell fire. (*He exhales heavily.*) Well, what can you do? Are they born like that or what? Who let him take it?

QUEENIE. I've had the woman round from the Cubs. She knows all about it. She'll be back again.

ALBERT (*peremptorily to* HARRY). Come on! (*They move towards the door.* ALBERT *turns to* CHARLES.) Come on, gormless! Don't sit there!

(CHARLES, *tutting to himself, slips on his shoes as* ALBERT *takes the lavatory key and follows* HARRY *out through the door.*)

QUEENIE (*calling shrilly after* ALBERT *and* HARRY). I don't want it in here, you know!

CHARLES (*moving towards the door*). Shur-rup!

(CHARLES *moves out and joins* ALBERT *and* HARRY *in the yard as* QUEENIE *goes down into the cellar.* ALBERT *opens the lavatory door. The three stand silent for a moment, lost in awe and admiration of the lectern.*)

ALBERT. By bloody hell! It's a big 'un!

HARRY (*proudly reiterating*). I'm driving along. I see it in my head-lights. I didn't know what it was.

CHARLES (*peremptorily*). You know what it is now, don't you?

ALBERT. Come on!

(ALBERT *moves into the lavatory and the three of them begin to manipulate the lectern out. They work without speaking except for a warning word from* ALBERT.)

Mind its beak!

(CHARLES *and* HARRY *now hold the lectern in the yard.* ALBERT *closes, but does not lock, the lavatory door and strolls with elaborate nonchalance to the end of the yard, where he takes a careful glance up and down the street. Seeing a neighbour somewhere he hails him with laborious cheerfulness.*)

Now then, Leonard!

(ALBERT *watches the neighbour out of sight and then his hypo-critical grin fades as he makes a quick gesture to* CHARLES *and* HARRY. *The three of them quickly transport the lectern into the house and close the door. The lectern is again set down in the centre of the floor.* CHARLES, ALBERT *and* HARRY *inspect the lectern for damage in transit.* HARRY, *seeing a tiny scratch on a wing, wets a finger and rubs the mark. They again admire the bird. It is obvious that to them it is a thing of beauty and that—a rare occasion in their lives—they are thinking in terms of beauty.*)

CHARLES. You know where that would look all right? (*He pauses.*) In somebody's garden.

(*There is a pause while they consider this attractive suggestion.*)

HARRY (*regretfully rejecting the suggestion*). It warps does wood though, doesn't it?

ALBERT. I'll tell you where that ought to be—in a hall. In a big hall in one of these big houses.

(*The cellar door bursts open as* QUEENIE *enters swinging a small sack of staples. She throws it on to the floor and some of the staples spill out.*)

QUEENIE. And you get rid of these as well. (*She glances at the lectern.*) It's no use bringing it in here.

(ALBERT, CHARLES *and* HARRY, *still admiring the lectern, glance at her in irritation and then turn their attention back to the lectern.*)

I'm going to start searching you lot before you come in at night.

(*Her voice tails off as she realizes that she has not got an audience. She moves closer and then she, too, is admiring the lectern.*) Shall I tell you where that'd look nice? On a shiny floor in a big mansion. (*With careful enunciation.*) In the hall.

ALBERT (*with approval*). What have I just said?

QUEENIE (*softly*). You don't see many lovely things these days. (*Stroking the lectern.*) Look at its feathers—there's every one picked out. You see, they don't bother these days. (*Regretfully she gives up her image of beauty and comes briskly back to earth.*) Anyway, you get it moved.

(ALBERT *looks first towards the bedroom stairs and then at the cellar door. Without a word he crosses and opens the cellar door wide and* HARRY *and* CHARLES *pick up the lectern and move towards the cellar door.*)

It won't go down there.

ALBERT. 'course it will!

(HARRY *and* CHARLES *carry the lectern down the cellar steps.* ALBERT *follows them and the door closes behind them.*)

QUEENIE (*complacently*). I'm telling them—it won't go round that bend.

(QUEENIE *looks down at the staples which have fallen out of the sack. She kneels and begins slowly picking them up.* DEANNA *and* DESMOND *march briskly into the yard from the street,* DEANNA *lagging slightly behind. They have obviously been having an argument.* DESMOND *walks straight up to the lavatory and opens the door.* DEANNA *watches him. He leaves the door open.*)

DEANNA. There's nothing in there, I've told you.

DESMOND. All right. Well, we'll go ask him where he's moved it to.

(DEANNA *bars his way.*)

DEANNA. Oh no you don't.

(DESMOND, *realizing he has got the upper hand, makes a generous gesture of despair.*)

DESMOND. Well—I'm not going to stand out here all day, am I!

DEANNA. Where are you going to go, then?

DESMOND (*with a half-embarrassed laugh*). It's up to you, isn't it? I mean, I'm not bothered what I do. I mean, I can go to the pub. See my mates.

DEANNA. Yes, I know. Spread it all round. You would.

DESMOND (*shrugging*). What else can we do?

DEANNA (*with elaborate unconcern*). I don't know. Go somewhere. Sit down. Have a talk.

DESMOND. Where?

(*After an uncertain pause,* DEANNA *comes to a decision. She walks up to the end of the yard and—like* ALBERT *before her—glances up and down the street.*)

DEANNA. Come on.

> (DESMOND *follows her.* DESMOND *and* DEANNA *move off into the street.* QUEENIE, *who has now finished picking up the staples, rises as the cellar door opens and* ALBERT *enters the room.*)

ALBERT. It won't go round that bend.

QUEENIE (*sarcastically*). Well, you surprise me now. I only told you fifteen times.

> (CHARLES *and* HARRY *enter from the cellar manipulating the lectern back into the room without difficulty. The lectern is returned to its position in the centre of the room.*)

HARRY. I'll tell you where it will go—we could get it up them bed-room steps.

CHARLES. You can take it yourself then. I'm not rupturing myself.

QUEENIE (*reluctantly*). We can't have it up there. They always search bedrooms. Always. First place they look.

ALBERT (*defeated*). It won't go downstairs—you won't have it upstairs—it can't stop here!

> (QUEENIE *looks at the lectern again admiringly and with longing.*)

QUEENIE (*now regretful*). No. It can't stop here.

CHARLES (*also regretful*). I mean, it's too big to keep, isn't it?

HARRY. What makes me mad is if we take it back it'll only get pinched again. Somebody else'll have it.

ALBERT. We'll have to dump it somewhere. (*Moving towards the front door.*) Come on, let's get them van doors open.

> (HARRY *and* ALBERT *go out into the street, leaving the front door open.* QUEENIE, *taking her glance reluctantly from the lectern, looks at the clock on the mantelpiece.* CHARLES *sits in his usual chair by the fire.*)

QUEENIE. What time does that Saturday picture-house club chuck out?

CHARLES (*still intent on the bird*). He can't dump it where he found it. They'll be watching that waste ground.

QUEENIE (*ignoring him*). 'cause he should be home by now. He daredn't come home, that's what it is.

CHARLES. Well, if he doesn't get that paint for me before one o'clock he'll know about it.

QUEENIE. Never mind your paint. He goes to the cobbler's before he goes anywhere.

> (QUEENIE'S *speech is cut short as* ALBERT *suddenly thrusts* DEANNA *violently into the room. He concentrates his voice so that it is quiet and vehement.*)

ALBERT. Get in! Get in that house! (*Thumping her on the back.*) You mucky bitch!

QUEENIE (*amazed*). What's up?

(ALBERT *ignores this as he leans out of the door and shouts up the street.*)

ALBERT. Get hold of him, then! And give him one for me! (*Turning to* QUEENIE.) Ask her what's up!

(QUEENIE *looks inquiringly at* DEANNA, *who is flustered and angry.*)

DEANNA. I'm leaving this house! I'm going to get a flat on my own!

(ALBERT *approaches her menacingly.*)

ALBERT. You want to be in a flat! We know what kind of a flat you'll be in! You mucky bitch!

DEANNA. Don't you dare hit me!

ALBERT. I'll do more than hit you! (*His immediate temper gives way to disgust.*) You're not worth hitting. (*To* QUEENIE.) We open them van doors. We hears a noise. (*He points dramatically at* DEANNA.) She's only on the bloody floor with a bloody bloke. Stretched out.

DEANNA (*defensively*). We weren't doing anything.

ALBERT (*ignoring her*). She was! Flat on her back with him! (*He takes hold of* DEANNA *and spins her round.*) Look at her! All dust on her back! Bits of sacking!

(HARRY *enters breathing heavily.* ALBERT *turns to him, releasing* DEANNA.)

Did you get him?

HARRY. He was up that street like a shot rabbit.

ALBERT (*to* QUEENIE, *in sheer astonishment*). Saturday morning, if you don't mind! Broad daylight! Why doesn't she lie down in the middle of the road with him? Like a couple of dogs? (*His anger gives way to hard-pressed invention.*) She wants to get down to town with him. Middle of Market Street. Opposite the bus queue. (*Laughing with comic incredulity.*) I tell you, bloody broad daylight! (*With a sudden reversion to his original mood, he swings round and slaps* DEANNA *across the face, to her own, and everyone else's complete surprise.*)

QUEENIE (*quietly and with satisfaction*). She asked for that. (*Turning to* HARRY.) And, in future, you keep them van doors locked—or better still keep it right away. Keep it out of the street. Leave it at work where it belongs. I knew what'd happen. How can you expect a lass to look after herself and behave herself when there's an empty van outside. God damn it all, it's asking for trouble is that.

HARRY. Don't blame her, blame him. He took her in there. I tell you, if he shows up in this street again I'll cripple him.

ALBERT. We've heard that tale before, whose fault is it. She must have led him on. She must have encouraged him. (*He regards* DEANNA *who has been sobbing helplessly. He shoves her with rough kindliness and speaks gruffly.*) Go on! Get that muck brushed off your back. You dozy bitch.

DEANNA. We weren't doing anything. (*She crosses and takes a clothes brush from a set on the wall and begins awkwardly brushing her back with little effect.*)

ALBERT (*dismissing the subject*). I don't know—it defeats me. (*He picks up the sack of staples and speaks to* HARRY.) We'll sling it down that quarry, that's the best place.

(ALBERT *goes out into the street with the sack of staples.* QUEENIE, *who has crossed to join* DEANNA, *takes the brush from her.*)

QUEENIE. Give us it here, lass! (QUEENIE *begins brushing* DEANNA'S *back vigorously.*) Well, you can't say you didn't ask for that from your dad, 'cause you did. You sit up and beg for trouble, you do.

DEANNA (*bitterly*). Just let him hit me again, that's all!

QUEENIE. But you ask for it, love! God Almighty, nobody begrudges you a bit of kissing and cuddling—but why can't you wait till night-time?

(*As* DEANNA *continues,* ALBERT *re-enters. He carries a couple of folded, empty sacks which he drops by the doorway. He wedges the door open in preparation for carrying out the lectern.*)

DEANNA. I wasn't leading anybody on. I only went into that van for one reason. And that's because of what he was going to say if I didn't.

QUEENIE. How do you mean, what he was going to say?

DEANNA (*nodding towards the lectern*). About that thing.

ALBERT (*incensed, interrupting*). You'd no right to tell him about the bloody bird!

DEANNA. That's just it. I didn't tell him. He got it off Jakie. He was going to spread it all round. He will do now, as well.

(CHARLES *gets up and walks across to the cellar door, where his jacket is hanging.*)

CHARLES. Get it out. It's brought nothing but trouble since it came.

HARRY. It's all right you saying get it out! What about helping us to shift it?

CHARLES (*angrily, as he pulls on his jacket*). I'm not shifting it. You fetched it in, you can get it out again!

HARRY. You're bone idle, that's your trouble.

(CHARLES *swiftly combs his hair in front of the mirror.*)

CHARLES. I've got more to do with my time. (*Angrily to* QUEENIE.) Where's our rotten Rory? He should have been here half an hour ago. I've got to go get that paint myself now.

(CHARLES *marches out of the house as* QUEENIE *calls after him.*)

QUEENIE. No paint! We don't need any paint! (*Appealing to* ALBERT.) Where's his common sense? We're getting one load of trouble out and he's bringing another load of trouble in!

ALBERT (*absentmindedly, nodding towards the lectern*). They can't trace paint. It's this swining thing I'm worried about.

QUEENIE. They can trace anything! (*Vaguely.*) It's all serial numbers.

ALBERT. Never mind serial numbers. Where's our Rory? It's him we want to trace. I'll put a serial number across his backside, then he'll know about it.

(QUEENIE *and* HARRY *follow* ALBERT's *gaze to the lectern. In spite of themselves there is some feeling of pride at* RORY's *achievement in being involved in such an awesome theft.*)

HARRY. He's a devil.

QUEENIE. He's an imp.

ALBERT. He's a little demon. And where the hell is he? You should have kept him in.

QUEENIE. I don't know where he is.

ALBERT. You shouldn't let him out at all. You want to keep him strapped to that bed.

DEANNA. He was up by the Regal half an hour ago. Him and another lad. Because I told him to get off home. Do you know what he was doing? They'd been to see this frogman picture. He was lying in the middle of the road, pretending to swim.

(ALBERT *dismisses* RORY *as he crosses to the lectern.*)

ALBERT. Oh, well, he'll be bloody run over by now. (*Glancing from the lectern to the door, he begins to size up the task of getting it out into the van. He addresses* HARRY *as he takes hold of the lectern.*) Just have a skeg out, see if there's anybody looking.

(HARRY *crosses to the open door and peers along the street. He recognizes somebody coming and nods to* ALBERT. *He steps aside as* JAKIE *arrives at the door.* JAKIE, *seeing* HARRY, *feels obliged to enter the house.* JAKIE *is received in dangerous silence.* HARRY *closes the door and stands with his back to it.* JAKIE, *sensing the atmosphere and realizing what has caused it, attempts to ingratiate himself with the family. He punctuates his speech with dry nervous laughs.*)

JAKIE (*indicating the lectern*). It is a big 'un, isn't it? Tall. Very tall. I didn't know they looked like that. 'course I never was a big church-goer. (*The others regard him coldly and he feels obliged to go on talking.*) Well, I hear you didn't get my chest of drawers, after all? She didn't tell Sidney Jeffries, did she? Well, she's let me down. No, only it just slipped out. I wouldn't have said anything. I wouldn't have breathed a word. Voluntarily. Only I was just asking her if I could use her lavatory. 'cause, I says, I can't get in ours. And then

it just slipped out. (*With well-simulated indignation.*) She didn't tell
Harry Chandler, did she? 'cause I didn't tell him. She must have
told him. I've told one person and that's her.

> (ALBERT *moves slowly and menacingly towards* JAKIE. JAKIE, *now
> almost in a panic, makes a last desperate bid to ingratiate himself. He
> pulls an official-looking document from his pocket and waves it in the
> air.*)

Have you got one of these, then? Has yours come? They're all
getting them, you know. They're coming round with them. From
the Housing.

> (QUEENIE *snatches the document from* JAKIE *and reads in silence
> for a few seconds.*)

QUEENIE (*still looking at the document she reacts with simple pleasure and
surprise*). Well, I am surprised. I thought they'd never get round
to us.

JAKIE. They start next week, that's the funny part. They don't give
you much warning.

QUEENIE (*ignoring* JAKIE *and quoting the document*). Slum Clearance.
Stage Four. (*Reacting with near hysterical joy.*) It's next week! We're
going to be out next week!

ALBERT. God Almighty! They don't give you much notice. It's like
shifting cattle.

JAKIE. Have you seen where they're sending us?

> (QUEENIE, *still intent on the document, ignores* JAKIE *again.*
> ALBERT, *interested, crosses to look at the document but* QUEENIE *holds
> up her hand to stop him.*)

QUEENIE. Hey, we're not going to Belle Isle estate. Hey, do you know
where they're sending us! Right out to Moorfields!

ALBERT (*grabbing the document from her*). You what! Moorfields!
(*Pointing dramatically.*) It'll take me an hour and a half to get to
work every morning!

DEANNA. That's Mecca dancing finished for me, that is. Last bus
goes at ten o'clock to Moorfields.

ALBERT (*despairingly*). Moorfields!

HARRY. I shan't get that van home at night-time. It'll take a gallon
of petrol to get out there.

ALBERT. Why don't they ship us all down to London and have done
with it.

> (OLD JAKIE, *who has been eagerly looking from one to another, is
> still sycophantic.*)

JAKIE. They send you anywhere they like.

QUEENIE (*with growing wonder*). Well, I don't care how far it is, because
they're lovely houses. They're beautiful houses up there.

DEANNA. There's no amusements! It's like a graveyard, there.

QUEENIE. It's beautiful. Because it's not like Belle Isle estate, you know. It's not just houses. It's not like these old estates. (*Waving her hands lyrically*.) It's all lawns and big gardens and all green. They've got it all laid out. And they're lovely houses. And you get a street, a little street with its own greens, and every house is different. And whatever window you look out of, you can see a tree. They make a special point of it. And every one of them houses has got a garden front and back. They've all got four bedrooms.

JAKIE. Well, how will I go on? I don't want four bedrooms.

QUEENIE (*now warming to* JAKIE *in her enthusiasm*). You won't, love. They've got them big blocks of flats for such as you. For single people. Well, it tells you, on your paper—where you've got to live.

ALBERT (*reading*). No. 77. Priory House. He'll fall down the bloody lift-shaft.

QUEENIE. Oh, you! You've not been there, Albert. You've not been round that estate. It's not ordinary, you know? It's not like an ordinary council estate! They're like bought houses.

ALBERT (*half won over*). Yes, well. They will be like bought houses by the time we've paid them rents.

QUEENIE. It's worth it. Because it's worth it just to have the fresh air. Our Rory'll be in his element there. There's all them fields. There's no muck and rubbish, there's no mischief to get into. He'll be as brown as a berry. He'll be a different lad.

(JAKIE *has now gained courage from the changed attitude towards him*.)

JAKIE. I've been looking for your Rory. I thought you were going to lend him to me this morning.

(ALBERT, *reminded of* JAKIE's *indiscretion, gives him a look.* JAKIE *moves rather rapidly towards the door*.)

Anyway, I shan't wait. Only I've got Mrs. Walton to tell. I don't think she's heard yet.

(ALBERT *hands him back the document*.)

ALBERT. And make sure that's all you do tell her. Don't go gabbing about anything else that doesn't concern you. Now, I'm warning you!

JAKIE (*as he fumbles at the door catch*). You can rely on me. (*He goes out*.)

ALBERT. Silly old twat!

DEANNA. Anyway, there's one good thing. He won't be in and out of the new house, borrowing keys. At least we'll have a lavvy to ourselves.

HARRY. No going outside. Hey, I'll tell you what we'll have in that back garden. We'll have a shed. Keep all our tools in it, get some woodwork done. You need to occupy your time, there.

(QUEENIE *begins looking around the room, examining her belong-ings. She speaks rather absently to* HARRY.)

QUEENIE. There's one thing you can make straight away, and that's a rustic seat—for that garden. (*Pondering.*) I'm sorry it's such short notice. I'd have liked to have moved in with all new furniture—I was setting my heart on it. We'll have to make do.

DEANNA (*nodding towards the chairs and sofa*). We can make some loose covers. Get some material.

QUEENIE. Curtains we'll have to buy. Stair-carpet. New bed for our Rory. Because he is not going into that house with that mattress. Lampshades. Bath things!

DEANNA. Ooh, are we going to get a new living-room carpet?

ALBERT. Nay, lass, we can't get everything all at once!

QUEENIE. Lino, you see! You never thought of that, did you? It all takes money. No, we'll get some lino down. (*Pointing down to the rugs.*) And we'll make do with these. Then later on we'll get a proper carpet. Maroon. I've wanted a maroon carpet. And we'll get all new furniture bit by bit as we go along.

ALBERT. That paint'll come in useful. You see, you didn't want to have it, did you? We'll get all the decorating done with that.

HARRY. All you'll be decorating is a bloody cell—in Dartmoor, mate. (*Indicating the lectern.*) 'cause we've still got Woody Woodpecker here, if you did but know it.

ALBERT (*galvanized into action*). Right! (*To* QUEENIE *as he crosses to the door and props it open.*) And as soon as we get back we're going to sit down and make a list of all we'll need.

QUEENIE. Spades we'll need, seeds, plants, rakes, forks—whatever else we have we want a lovely garden.

(ALBERT *and* HARRY *pick up the lectern as* QUEENIE *continues with an expansive sweep of her arm.*)

With a big sweeping lawn. (*She watches* HARRY *and* ALBERT *in silence as they move towards the door with the lectern. She calls out urgently.*) Wait!

(ALBERT *and* HARRY *put down the lectern and look at* QUEENIE.) (*Rather softly.*) I just want to picture that bird on that lawn.

(ALBERT *and* HARRY *step back and, with* QUEENIE *and* DEANNA, *examine the lectern from a new angle. There is a silence of several seconds.*)

DEANNA. It's a long way out, is Moorfields. It's not near, like Belle Isle.

HARRY. 'course, it's a different Police Force as well. It's the County, is that. They don't deal with City cases.

QUEENIE (*again describing with her hands*). I can just see it. Standing up on that lawn. A little flower bed underneath.

ALBERT. Crocuses.

(With one accord the family makes up its mind. QUEENIE crosses and bangs the door shut as HARRY and ALBERT pick up the lectern and move it back towards the centre of the room. DEANNA moves to pick up the sacks from the floor.)

QUEENIE. We'll have a beautiful garden!

CURTAIN

ACT THREE

Late afternoon of the same day. Although the street lamp is lit in the yard, it is still light; the dusk draws close. In the living-room the table is, as usual, cluttered, but now with the remnants of tea. The lectern now stands in its central position, but on a couple of spread-out newspapers. On the floor there are several very large cans of paint. HARRY holds a can of blue paint while CHARLES, with a small brush, is meticulously painting the lectern. QUEENIE is watching them with interest. She then looks up at the clock anxiously. DEANNA is kneeling by the sideboard. She has one of the sideboard drawers on the floor beside her and is sorting through its contents, rejecting obsolete items such as old ties, a cardigan, broken box camera, etc. CHARLES and HARRY work in silence for a moment. A desultory argument has been going on between them.

HARRY. I'll tell you another way of getting there.

CHARLES (*intent on his work*). Shur-rup!

HARRY. No, well, you've said there's only one. Well, I've told you two ways already and I'll tell you another. 36A.

DEANNA (*looking up*). 36A goes up Lane End Road. It doesn't go anywhere near Moorfields.

HARRY. I'm telling you. You go up Lane End Road. You go up Lane End Road as far as the clock, then you walk across. You walk right across Lane End Park and I'll tell you where it brings you out. It brings you out at that water tower. Well, you get a Number 18 from there. Only two stops—then all you've got to do is walk on. You walk on till you come to that new road that they're making—and that takes you right into Moorfields.

QUEENIE (*edgily*). Oh, shut up, Harry! (HARRY *gives* QUEENIE *a surprised look and she justifies herself by looking at the clock again.*) I wish that lad was home. He's had no dinner, he's had no tea.

CHARLES. Well, whose fault's that?

QUEENIE. I don't know—

HARRY (*unconcernedly*). He's run away again. I'll tell you, if he knows he's going to get thumped when he comes home he won't turn up till midnight.

CHARLES. He'll be in that brickfield. Where he always goes. Same as that time he spilt that bottle of ink down his trousers—daredn't come home.

QUEENIE (*with fond reminiscence*). I nearly killed him. I thought he had concussion! Then it turns out it wasn't him who spilled it, that was the funny part.

(*There are some moments of silence while the family is lost in the pleasant memory of the incident. During the following scene* QUEENIE *rises and crosses silently out of the house and into the yard, where she rummages in the dustbin.*)

HARRY (*to* CHARLES). Do you know what I'm going to start doing when we get up to Moorfields?

CHARLES. What?

HARRY (*in a tone of considerable surprise at himself*). I'm going to start playing football! I'm fed up of going down to that pub every night.

CHARLES (*ignoring this and speaking to* DEANNA). Can you get flower bulbs where you work, our lass?

DEANNA. Only if you knock them off from the Welfare.

CHARLES. Well, can you get us some? I'd be good at gardening.

HARRY (*following his own train of thought*). No, 'cause they've got a team—Moorfields Old Boys. You're supposed to have gone to the school. Well, they've got no check. I'll stick my name down, anyway.

CHARLES (*coming up with a revolutionary idea*). You can buy bulbs anyway. If you can't get me some crocus bulbs I'll go down and buy some. I'll pay for them.

DEANNA. You're not going to dig all that garden up, 'cause we want that lawn. I'm going to sit out there and sun-bathe.

(QUEENIE, *who has now unearthed from the dustbin the Cub uniform, moves back along the yard and pauses at the end to call down the street.*)

QUEENIE. Rory? . . . Rory!

(*There being no reply,* QUEENIE *moves back into the house, where she crosses immediately to the brush set on the wall and, taking down a brush, begins to clean the uniform.*)

CHARLES (*impatiently referring to his paint brush*). All the bloody bristles are coming out. Where's all them brushes I fetched home?

QUEENIE. They're still in that box in the cellar, aren't they? I thought you were going to sell them.

HARRY. What, them brushes? Our old lad sold them six months ago. Didn't he tell you?

CHARLES. He'd better not have done!

(CHARLES, *indignant, rushes out through the cellar door. Over the next few lines of dialogue* DESMOND *arrives in the street and moons indecisively in the yard, occasionally peering round the corner towards the door of the house.*)

HARRY (*to* DEANNA). He did! He sold them in the Builders Arms to that Indian fellow that comes in with a suitcase. I was there! (*A *new thought strikes him and he turns to* QUEENIE.) Hey! He'll go a bit short when we get up there, won't he? He'll have to give up waiting on.

QUEENIE. Oh, no! Oh, no. There's a beautiful pub up there. The Ringway. They're always short-staffed. There's that big concert room—well, you get tips there. You see, you don't have to fiddle; they give you tips. (QUEENIE *has now finished brushing the Cub uniform. She glances at it approvingly.*) He can join the Cubs up there. And there'll be much nicer lads for him to play with.

(QUEENIE *crosses and goes to the bedroom stairs.* DESMOND, *in the yard, gives a whistle which is obviously recognized by* DEANNA *as a mating call.* DEANNA *looks up as the whistle is repeated. She glances across at* HARRY *in some little panic, but* HARRY, *who is stirring the paint, has not noticed.* DEANNA *crosses and takes the lavatory key from its nail.*)

DEANNA. I'm just going to the lavvy.

HARRY (*in some surprise*). Well, you can manage by yourself, can't you?

(DEANNA *goes out into the yard. During the first few lines of the following scene* HARRY *saunters out and into the cellar.*)

DEANNA (*approaching* DESMOND). Our Harry's in, you know. He'll kill you if he comes out here.

DESMOND (*with assumed indifference*). He'll have to kill me, then, won't he?

DEANNA. Where did you go, then? When you ran away?

DESMOND (*defensively*). I wasn't running away. There were two of them, wasn't there? Your Harry and your old man. I'll take either of them on—one at a time.

DEANNA (*dryly*). Bet you would.

DESMOND. I would!

(*There is a short silence and then* DEANNA *giggles to herself.*)

DEANNA. I can just see their faces when they opened that van. He hit me, you know—me dad.

DESMOND (*interested*). Did he?

DEANNA. He clouted me across the face.

DESMOND (*suddenly serious*). I wasn't going to—you know. I mean, if you didn't want me to.

DEANNA. Well, I said I didn't want you to, didn't I?

DESMOND (*understandingly*). You couldn't very well say anything else, could you? Only, I mean, I wasn't really going to tell anybody about that bird, if you didn't. I haven't told anybody, you know.

DEANNA. It's all the same to me whether you have or you haven't.

DESMOND. Well, I haven't.

DEANNA (*again giggling with reminiscence*).   I don't know what my mother thinks—I had all straw all down my back. All muck.

DESMOND.   It's your dress, isn't it? (*He adds a clumsy endearment.*) Anyway—you shouldn't have been wearing a dress.

> (DEANNA *takes this as a compliment and acknowledges it with silence and downcast eyes.* DESMOND *recognizes her silence as encouragement.*)

(*Hesitantly.*) You should have taken it off. (*He pauses.*) You should have let me take it off for you.

> (DESMOND *has now gone too far.* DEANNA *rebukes him roughly but kindly.*)

DEANNA.   Don't be cheeky.

> (DESMOND *accepts the rebuke, but the silence that follows is not an uncomfortable one.*)

DESMOND.   What are you doing tonight, then?

DEANNA.   Don't know. Stopping in.

DESMOND.   Why don't you go out with me, then?

DEANNA.   I was out with you last night.

DESMOND.   Do you want to go with me tomorrow night, then?

DEANNA (*she considers*).   All right. I'll go out with you tomorrow night.

DESMOND.   Why won't you go out with me tonight, then?

DEANNA (*reconsidering*).   All right. I'll go out with you tonight. (*Her voice suddenly harshens with possessiveness.*) Hey, and listen you! Do you still go dancing with Doreen Chapman?

DESMOND (*lying*).   No!

DEANNA (*thumping him on the shoulder*).   Well, don't! (*The point made, she reverts to her gentler tones.*) Where we going tonight?

DESMOND (*making a joke*).   Back of that van.

> (*They laugh together and they are very close. He kisses her without any of the usual mauling. The absence of this sexual byplay is such a rare experience for them both that the kiss becomes for them an intense sexual experience.* DEANNA *clings to* DESMOND, *who is caressing her face. They speak softly and the everyday trivialities become great intimacies.*)

DEANNA (*softly*).   You've got soft hands.

DESMOND (*justifying what he feels is a fault*).   Yeh. Well, you've got to wear these special gloves in my job.

DEANNA.   I pass your place every morning, you know.

DESMOND.   Yeh, I know.

DEANNA.   I once saw you. You were standing in that gateway.

DESMOND.   Just outside the Carbon Room. You want to wave the next time you see me.

> (DEANNA's *mind moves on to other things and the intimacy is lost.*)

DEANNA.   I shan't be going that way much longer.

DESMOND. No, none of us will. Has that Housing fellow been yet?

DEANNA. No, he's been to most of them, but he hasn't been to us yet. When are they moving you? Next Wednesday?

DESMOND. No, Thursday.

DEANNA. We might live next door to each other—you never know.

DESMOND. Yeh. I wasn't looking forward to going up Belle Isle, but I am now.

DEANNA (*with fear in her voice*). We're not going to Belle Isle, we're going to Moorfields.

DESMOND. Who? All our street's going to Belle Isle.

DEANNA. All our street's going to Moorfields.

DESMOND. Ah, well—that's bloody marvellous, that is.

DEANNA. I'm glad we're not going to Belle Isle. I hate that estate. There's no grass, there's nothing.

DESMOND. That puts the tin lid right on it, that does. (*His voice rising aggrievedly.*) I can't charge over to stinking Moorfields from that bloody hole every night. You've got to change buses sixty-four times.

DEANNA. It's right over the other side, isn't it?

DESMOND. And I mean you can't get back home again. You get stuck in Moorfields after nine o'clock at night and you might as well kip down on the cricket pitch. Because you won't get a bus back.

DEANNA. I know.

(*They both realize that the affair that was blossoming between them is becoming a geographical impossibility.*)

DESMOND. It just makes my day, does this. (*He broods, seeking some solution to the problem.*) I mean, even if I meet you in town, I mean, you don't want to go home by yourself, do you?

DEANNA, Not on them late buses, I don't. Not with all them drunks that you get.

DESMOND. And there's Muggins here—I've been thinking, first lass I've met for ages who doesn't look like something the cat's brought in. Then she has to go and live up bloody Moorfields.

DEANNA (*shrugging*). Not my fault, is it?

DESMOND. Not mine either, is it?

DEANNA. Is Doreen Chapman going up Belle Isle?

DESMOND. I don't know. Suppose so. She lives in our street, doesn't she?

DEANNA. Oh, well, you won't go short then, will you?

(*Now* DESMOND *shrugs. Everything is destroyed. He walks up the yard as far as the street, and then back again. He regards* DEANNA, *his hands deep in his pockets. He is about to speak, but he changes his mind, shrugs, and then walks away down the street.* DEANNA *stands pensively by the wall.* ALBERT *approaches down the street and passes the yard in a hurry, calling out to* DEANNA *as he does so.*)

ALBERT. You don't want to be stood there!

(*He enters the living-room as* QUEENIE *comes down the stairs. Almost in the same breath* ALBERT *calls to* QUEENIE *as he switches on the light.*)

He's not in them brickfields!

QUEENIE (*drawing the curtains*). Oh dear me.

(DEANNA, *subdued, follows* ALBERT *into the house and hangs up the lavatory key.*)

ALBERT. I've looked. I've searched for him. (*Indignantly.*) I've been right up South Institution Road, I've been through them brickfields, I've been down that quarry.

QUEENIE (*puzzled rather than worried*). Well, where is he?

ALBERT. I don't know where he is. And listen. (*He indicates the lectern.*) We've not heard the last of that thing yet. There's two police knocking from door to door all down there. (*He waves dramatically in the direction of the street.*) There's a police car parked outside St. Christopher's, and there's that Cub woman talking to a detective. I'll tell you who it is as well. It's Detective-sergeant McIntyre—him that came about that lead piping, that time.

(*Over the above* CHARLES *and* HARRY *have emerged from the cellar and picked up on the last few sentences of the conversation.* CHARLES *is carrying a new, cellophane-covered paint-brush.*)

QUEENIE. Ooh, he's a nasty cow, he is. He's that sarky one, isn't he?

ALBERT. I tell you, they're going from door to door!

(HARRY *moves rapidly over to the lectern and picks up a paint-brush.*)

HARRY. Come on, let's get this job finished.

ALBERT (*incensed at* HARRY'S *stupidity*). What you talking about, it's no use bloody painting it! What will it look like when you've painted it! You're not going to tell me a detective-sergeant isn't going to recognize it! Hell's bells, we know they're not bright, but they're not bloody lunatics! What's he going to think it is, then, when you've painted it! Paint it—you're not right in the head. (*His indignation having run down slightly, it is given a fresh impetus as a new thought strikes him, and his voice rises again.*) What's it going to look like, when you've painted it—a bloody donkey? It's a bird! It's a bird! You can paint it six times over, it's still a bloody bird!

HARRY (*also angry*). Don't shout at me! Who do you think you're talking to!

ALBERT. Shout at you—you want shouting at, you do! They're knocking on the doors! What will they see, first thing? There's fifteen gallons of paint there, knocked off! Anybody can see it's knocked off! (*Rounding on* CHARLES *as he is now almost incoherent.*) What did you fetch—she told you not to fetch it in!

QUEENIE.   Well, don't stand there yacking and yammering and screaming and yelling—what are we going to do, that's what we want to know.

DEANNA.   What's wrong with putting it down in the cellar?

CHARLES.   Shur-rup, dozy! It won't go in the cellar.

HARRY.   We were fighting it on them cellar steps for half an hour.

DEANNA.   Well, I didn't know, did I!

ALBERT.   No, we know you didn't know—you were flat on your back in that van. Rolling about! (*He whips round to* CHARLES *and* HARRY *and begins to speak urgently.*) Now listen! First thing, we get it covered up. Second thing, it goes in that van. Third thing, it stops in that van, and it stops in that van until we get in that new house, safe.

HARRY.   I can't have it in that van!

ALBERT.   It's going in that van. The paint's going in that van. That bacon's going in that van. Them liquorice allsorts you fetched home are going in that van.

HARRY.   It's the firm's van, it's not my van! How can I get a day's work done with my van stuffed up with birds and bacon and paint and God knows what else? It'll look like a travelling shop!

DEANNA.   Will it go in the bedrooms?

QUEENIE.   You talk to yourself here. It does not go in them bedrooms.

CHARLES.   I'll tell you where—

ALBERT (*cutting him short and taking command*).   Now shut up, the lot of you. (*He begins barking orders which move the others into action. To* HARRY.) Sacks. (*To* CHARLES.) Paint. (*To* DEANNA.) And you. Get out and find our Rory and don't come back till you've found him.

　　　(HARRY *begins draping the lectern with the sacks which lie on the floor.* CHARLES *begins putting lids on cans of paint.* QUEENIE *moves across to help* HARRY.)

DEANNA.   He won't come home with me. He never does.

ALBERT.   You fetch him home, you drag him back. Because if one of them police catches him wandering about, the whole lot'll come out. Go look on that recreation ground.

　　　(DEANNA, *taking her coat from behind the door, calls to* ALBERT *as she goes out.*)

DEANNA.   He won't come with me, you know.

QUEENIE.   Tell him I say he's got to.

　　　(*The door closes behind* DEANNA *and we see her move off along the street.* ALBERT *crosses and helps* CHARLES *with the paint.*)

He'll be black bright when he comes in. If he's been down in that recreation ground—all that cinder dust.

ALBERT (*mildly*). He'll be sky-blue-bloody-pink-with-yellow-dots-on when I've finished with him.

QUEENIE. Then you wonder why he runs off. You see, I've been thinking tonight. And I think we hit that lad too much, between us. It's all right one hitting him, but he gets it twice over.

ALBERT. We've got to knock some sense into him, lass.

QUEENIE. Well, I know, but you can have too much of a good thing. You see what happened last Sunday when I heard about him melting that lard down in the fire? Well, I hit him—I chased him down that street with a shoe. Well, nobody told me you'd belted him already. He got it twice over.

ALBERT. It won't hurt him. (*Pointing to* HARRY.) Look at him. He's all right. (*To* HARRY.) How many times did I thump you when you were little? (*To* QUEENIE.) He's bad enough now. What would he have been like without a few good hidings. He'd have been hung for murder.

QUEENIE. Yes, well, you just listen to what I'm saying. We're just going to stop hitting him so much. And I'll tell you something else. He's going to the seaside this year. He's going to have a holiday. Build up his little legs.

ALBERT. He's all right! Once he gets running wild up in all them fields, comes home and gets a meal inside him, he'll be like Billy Bunter. And you want to start cooking proper meals when we get up there.

QUEENIE. I shall do! 'cause they have lovely stoves. Eye-level grill. He'll have a cooked breakfast, he'll have a cooked dinner and he'll have a cooked tea—if he wants. Once I get going with the stove—

(QUEENIE *breaks off as there is a peremptory official rat-tat-tat on the door. The family freezes and look at each other.* ALBERT, *with a quick gesture of his hand, indicates that part of the lectern is not covered over.* HARRY *quickly adjusts the sacking.* QUEENIE *moves towards the door and* ALBERT *calls to her in an urgent hoarse whisper.*)

ALBERT. Here! Try not to let them in! (*Turning to* CHARLES *and indicating the cans of paint.*) You found this lot!

(QUEENIE *opens the door to disclose* DOUGLAS DOBSON, *who is standing outside. He is wearing a grubby raincoat and carries a large official-looking ledger which is crammed with various loose papers.* DOUGLAS *is poring into his book and does not look up as he speaks.*)

DOUGLAS. Twenty-three—Hesseltine.

QUEENIE (*nervously*). Yes?

DOUGLAS. Housing Department!

(*He says this in a sing-song voice which, quite rightly, he assumes to be an open sesame to the house. He marches in past* QUEENIE.)

QUEENIE. Oh. Oh! Oh! (*Her voice rises with relief.*) Come in, come in!

> (DOUGLAS *is already assembling papers on the table. He looks round benevolently.*)

DOUGLAS. I don't suppose you've got a Ritchie hidden away here, have you? By any remote chance?

QUEENIE (*considering the matter seriously*). Ritchie, Ritchie. No, there's no Ritchie in this street. There's Rushworth.

DOUGLAS. I've got Rushworth. I've had three-quarters of an hour with Rushworth. It's Ritchie that's my biggest problem. (*Comic indignation enters his voice.*) It's going to be a shambles on Wednesday! I tell you, they'll be going in all directions! There isn't a Ritchie! They've got him down for a flat. I bet he's been dead twenty years!

QUEENIE (*still serious*). We've been here since nineteen-thirty-seven, and we never knew anybody of that name.

DOUGLAS. I shall still be at it at midnight at this rate. But it's Wednesday I'm waiting for. (*The idea of the forthcoming migration is always something that appeals to* DOUGLAS'S *sense of humour, and again there is an undertone of hysterical laughter in his voice.*) Talk about D-Day! Charge of the Light Brigade won't be in it! You're moving on Wednesday, they're cutting the water off Monday night! Huh-hoo! You won't get a cup of tea for two days! They'll be flaking out in the street! Housing Committee! They're going to uproot and transplant an entire neighbourhood in one day, and they've got about as much idea as my backside. Oh dear. (*He mops his eyes and picks up a paper.*) Anyway, press on. (*He is again, for a moment, the official, as he reads from his book.*) Now. Let's see. Mr. Albert Hesseltine, Mrs. Queenie Hesseltine, you're the householders. Charles Hesseltine, Harry Lauder Hesseltine, Deanna Hesseltine, Rory Hesseltine. Have there been any additions to your family?

ALBERT (*jocular in his relief*). Isn't it enough for you?

> (DOUGLAS *looks at* ALBERT *for the first time and greets him civilly.*)

DOUGLAS. Good evening! (ALBERT *inclines his head.*) Ready for the Big Push, then?

> (ALBERT, *like his son* CHARLES, *does not like dealing with strangers. He shuffles with embarrassment and mumbles his reply.*)

ALBERT. Just getting ready.

DOUGLAS (*indicating the shrouded lectern*). I see you are.

QUEENIE (*quickly diverting his attention*). You'll have had a busy day, then.

DOUGLAS. Huh hoo! I've never had one like it in all my born days! There's an old woman down there, she thinks she's taking six cats with her! There's them across the road there—it's a case of "Can I carry on in business as a chimney sweep?" (*With great comic indignation.*) I says, "You can not carry on business as a chimney sweep!"

I says, "Where do you think you're going?" I says, "You're going to a council house. Those days are over, my friend!" I said. Then I'm chatting to another old fellow; he's telling me there's somebody keeps a big bird in the lavatory. I couldn't make out whether it was a swan or a goose or what they'd got hold of. I tell you, it's an education, just to walk into some of these houses. I don't know. (*Calming down.*) I do not know. Anyway. There's your official notification.

> (*He hands* QUEENIE *a document similar to the one which* JAKIE *had.* QUEENIE *holds it reverently in her hand.*)

QUEENIE. Thank you very much.

> (*As he continues,* DOUGLAS *plies* QUEENIE *with papers. Now that he is speaking in his official role again, he talks as though he were addressing a moron. It is a speech he has made many times before.*)

DOUGLAS. Now you've got your official notification. Now, these documents here are formal applications for your various public utilities.

QUEENIE. Oh yes.

DOUGLAS. Those must be signed. Must be. And returned to the various offices before Monday afternoon. (*Lapsing from his official role he again starts to become overwhelmed with comic indignation.*) And if you take my advice, don't post them, take them. It's not my job, lugging these round! It should have been done weeks ago! Nobody thought! I laugh. It's next Thursday morning I'm thinking about, because they'll be getting up, there'll be no gas, there'll be no light, there'll be no electricity, there'll be nothing. It'll be like bedlam up at Moorfields. I don't know. I do not know.

QUEENIE (*politely*). Well, you expect to be mucked about, don't you? It's getting in that's the main thing.

HARRY. Well, what arrangements have they made, for transport?

DOUGLAS. They've made no arrangements, that's what tickles me. That's the funny side of it! There's a hundred and three family units to be transported to various estates in one day. There's not the vans! They're scouring the countryside for removal vans!

HARRY. Oh, well, I can borrow a van from our firm, so we'll be all right.

DOUGLAS. I'm only glad to hear it. Because there's a colleague of yours across the street—nobody will move him, nobody! (*His voice again rises with near-hysterical laughter.*) He won't move! Flatly refuses! He's got six tons of coal in his cellar and he says he won't budge an inch without it! Can you see a removal man shovelling coal? Six tons of coal! I wouldn't care, but he's going to a smokeless zone! (*Calming down again.*) Never had a day like it!

> (QUEENIE *has been studying her "official notification" during the above.*)

QUEENIE. Excuse me. Excuse me.

(*Mopping his eyes,* DOUGLAS *gives her his attention.*)

DOUGLAS. Now then, is it something you don't understand?

QUEENIE. Well, I'm very sorry, but you've given us the wrong paper.

(DOUGLAS *takes the paper from her happily.*)

DOUGLAS. You don't surprise me.

(QUEENIE *continues as* DOUGLAS *studies the paper.*)

QUEENIE. You see, if you'll look, it says No. 75 Priory House.

DOUGLAS. Yes.

QUEENIE. Well, that's a flat, isn't it?

DOUGLAS. Yes?

QUEENIE (*formally*). You see, we've been under the impression that we're not going in a flat. We've been given to understand that we're going into a house.

DOUGLAS (*officially*). Well, whoever told you that had no authority to do so. We've none of us had any authority to tell anybody where they were going to live. Not till you received the official notification.

(ALBERT *walks menacingly across and takes the document from* QUEENIE. *He glances at it.*)

ALBERT (*tearing the paper in two and dropping it on the floor.*) You don't get me in a flat.

(ALBERT *walks calmly back to his previous position and stands with his back to* DOUGLAS. DOUGLAS *takes this rebellion with his hysterical amusement.*)

DOUGLAS. What the—you're all in flats, man! It's the modern age! It's the modern age! The whole streets in flats! (*Demonstrating with his hands.*) We're going to up-end this whole terrace. It's your whole mode of life. Instead of living next door to each other, you'll be living above and below each other. There's no more horizontal housing. Those days are gone, my friend!

ALBERT (*dogmatically*). You don't get me in a flat.

QUEENIE. There's hundreds of houses up there. Rows and rows of them. We were told quite specifically we were going in a house.

DOUGLAS. They'll tell you anything down there. There's a woman across the street, she can't get about—she's been labouring under the delusion she's getting a bungalow. They've put her on the twelfth storey! There's another fellow rambling on about what he's going to do and what he isn't going to do in his garden. I says, "Garden, garden, where did you get that tale from?" I says, "You've got your communal area." He says, "Can I dig it up?" I says, "Dig it up, they'll dig you up if you do!" It's all done for you! You're in flats now!

HARRY. What floor are we supposed to be on, then?

DOUGLAS. You've been allocated a flat on the eighth floor.

ALBERT. You don't get me on the eighth floor.

DOUGLAS (*blandly*). You'll go where you're put, my friend.

(ALBERT, *who has been seething underneath, suddenly turns on* DOUGLAS, *strides over and pushes him violently in the chest.*)

ALBERT. Don't you talk to me like that, you four-eyed get!

(DOUGLAS, *to whom assault is a common hazard of his job, is in no way put out by this. Blandly he begins to gather his papers together. There is the familiar amusement in his voice as he addresses* ALBERT.)

DOUGLAS. Well, that's a very fine start! I can see we shall get on very well together!

ALBERT (*still angry, flails his arms*). Go on! Get out! Get back to your town hall, you cissified get!

(DOUGLAS, *picking up his book, elaborately and still with apparent good humour, makes a note, reading it out as he does so.*)

DOUGLAS. Mr.—Hesseltine—difficult—tenant. (*He puts his pen away with a flourish and beams round.*) Right. I would just point out that I shall be your rent collector. My name is Mr. Dobson, and I shall be calling on Tuesday mornings. (*Now speaking with amiable viciousness.*) And I would just call your attention to the conditions of tenancy. (*He hands* ALBERT *an official-looking blue document.*) You will not deface any wall. You will not commit any nuisance of any description whatsoever. You will be jointly responsible for the neatness and cleanliness of the concrete landing. You will not suffer any child to play in the vicinity of the lifts. And, of course, we shall expect a clean rent-book. (*He flashes the family a bitter-sweet smile which they return with stone-faced hostility. He crosses to the door. He pauses and looks around the rather shabby, crowded room with ill-concealed amusement. He shakes his head.*) I don't know!

(DOUGLAS *goes out. We see him going across the top of the yard, still shaking his head and laughing to himself. In the living-room the silence is held for some moments.* QUEENIE *stoops and picks up the torn paper. Although* QUEENIE'S *words are mild, she speaks with an infinite sadness.*)

QUEENIE. Well, I am surprised tonight. I'm very surprised.

ALBERT (*bitterly and in defeat*). What did you expect. They're all the same. You might have known.

(ALBERT *walks over to the lectern and pulls off the sack which covers the head and wings of the carved bird. He stares at it dully.* QUEENIE *speaks quietly as she sits down by the table.*)

QUEENIE. It's a pity.

HARRY (*jerking his thumb in reference to* DOUGLAS). We're going to have some trouble with that one. If he's going to be round every Tuesday, poking his nose in.

CHARLES. Well, there is one good thing. If you do have any private stuff and there is somebody coming, you can always whip it in the lift and up to somebody else's floor. They can't trace it back.

HARRY. I'll tell you what I will tell you. You know that big main entrance? Well you can walk through there with what you like, because nobody knows which floor you're taking it to.

(QUEENIE, *who has been staring at the lectern, speaks softly.*)

QUEENIE. I could just have pictured it on that lawn. It was only a garden I wanted. I could just see it, with its wings all out, and a seat underneath, for us to sit on. (*She demonstrates the wings.*) And crocuses underneath, you know, like reaching up to it. (*She rises in a sudden gust of anger.*) I only wanted a bloody garden! Damn it all, it's not much to ask! We've only waited twenty-five years to get shifted out of this muckhole! Is it too much to ask, a bit of green for yourself!

CHARLES (*gruffly compassionate*). Well, you don't bother. It's always the same with this lot—if you want anything, get it yourself. We'll get you some flowers—we'll get you some flowers, out on the sill. If I can just get hold of some boxes—

HARRY. There's all them ammunition cases up at the Ordnance Depot. I go there twice a week—you don't worry about boxes.

CHARLES. There you are! We'll get you some flowers!

QUEENIE (*quietly*). I wanted that statue.

ALBERT. You've had that, Queenie lass. You can't have a thing like that in a block of flats.

QUEENIE. I know.

HARRY. We can't leave it here.

ALBERT. We can't take it out and dump it, now. It's too late.

CHARLES. What can we do with it?

QUEENIE. It's the most beautiful thing I've ever seen in my life.

ALBERT. We'll have to smash it up.

(*There is a long silence during which they continue to look at the lectern. Then, one by one, they avert their glances from it. They look at each other, almost in embarrassment. At which point DEANNA enters, quickly and out of breath.*)

DEANNA. He's not there! I've been twice round that recreation ground.

CHARLES. We've got more to bother about than him.

(*All of QUEENIE's old viciousness has now returned.*)

QUEENIE. I'll bother about him! As soon as he walks through that door I'll belt him round this room.

DEANNA. I've been to Mrs. Shepherd's and their Michael's been home two hours.

ALBERT. If I could just find out where he goes off to.

QUEENIE. When we get up there he goes off to nowhere. He stops in. I'm not having him out on that landing—chalking and playing and making his muck. (*Viciously round on* DEANNA.) And don't think you're living in a house, 'cause you're not. You're going to Priory House. And, listen you! If I catch you hanging round that staircase with lads I'll throw a bucket of cold water over you.

ALBERT (*to* DEANNA *in justification of* QUEENIE'S *anger*). Eighth-floor flat they've stuck us on! No garden. They won't give us a garden.

QUEENIE. And we can't take the bird with us.

CHARLES (*bitterly*). Did you ever really think we would be able to? Because it comes as no shock to me, I can tell you. I knew the minute he brought it in the house. You can't keep things like that.

HARRY. Well, it's the last thing of that sort I fetch home. I'm going to fetch home stuff we can use in future. Food. Ciggies. Stuff like that.

DEANNA. You can't have beautiful things, mother. Who do you think you are?

QUEENIE (*savagely*). Get the flamer chopped up!

> (*During the following speech* CHARLES *goes up to the lectern and begins assessing it as so much firewood, knocking it and rocking it to test the quality of the wood. He then goes off into the cellar.*)

ALBERT. I don't know why you didn't leave it where it was. Why didn't you leave it on that waste ground? It wasn't doing you any harm, was it?

HARRY (*stung*). No, and it wasn't doing you any harm, either. Don't you come at me. How did it get on the waste ground in the first place!

ALBERT. Little Lord Itchy-Fingers. I tell you, he's a bloody klepto-maniac, that one. What did he want to touch it for, that's what beats me! (*Suddenly amazed.*) Going into a church! Good God Almighty, I mean I could have understood it if it had been Bonfire Night! I mean, if he'd come home with a bottle of milk or a bar of chocolate. What did he want it for?

QUEENIE (*quietly, but ominously*). He needs a firm hand.

DEANNA. I expect he just liked the look of it.

> (*During the following speech* CHARLES *emerges from the cellar with a saw. He is wiping the blade with a piece of cloth.*)

ALBERT. It's no use hitting him. He needs more than hitting. He wants bringing to his senses. I've been soft with him. (*To* QUEENIE.) And so have you. And what have you been telling him about I'll make him a kite as soon as we move? (*With a malicious grin.*) He gets no kite. He gets nothing! (*Slowly and definitely.*) He—gets—nothing. All I require of him is that he keeps right out of my way. Alto-gether. Because every time he comes within arm's reach (*With a vicious swipe of the hand.*) he gets one. (*With another swipe.*) Right across the face.

> (*The conversation ends as* CHARLES, *with two clean rasps of the saw, makes his initial mark on the neck of the eagle. The family turn*

and look at him as CHARLES *pauses. They then swing round as there is a peremptory knock at the door and* JAKIE *shuffles in.*)

HARRY (*gasping with elaborate relief*). Can't you let people know when you're coming in? I thought it was the C.I.D.

ALBERT. He walks in as though he lived here.

JAKIE (*giving a short sycophantic laugh as he sizes up the situation*). You're getting rid of it, then?

CHARLES (*brusquely*). What's it look as if we're doing?

JAKIE. No, 'cause I was wondering—how you were going to go on. They're going to every house, you know. There's a sergeant and a constable—they're only in the next street.

DEANNA. Tell us news not history.

JAKIE (*feeling unwelcome, brings up another topic of conversation*). I hear you've got your paper then? (*They look at him coldly.*) I hear you're going into Priory House, same as me? What floor are you going to be on?

QUEENIE (*suspicion dawning upon her*). Eighth.

JAKIE (*triumphantly*). We'll be next door!

QUEENIE (*bearing her cross*). I might have known it.

JAKIE. Well, that's lucky that is. How we've come together. You see, there's one four-bedroom and one one-bedroom on every floor. It's the new policy, so that the old don't feel pushed out of it. Well, it is lucky is that.

(*These tidings are received in cold silence by the family.* CHARLES *turns and makes a further preliminary incision in the eagle's neck.* JAKIE *watches him with interest.*)

(*Again coming back to the subject of the lectern.*) No, well, I was wondering what you were going to do. See, I thought you'd locked it back in that lavatory. 'cause I was trying to get in an hour ago. I went down twice. I had to use Johnson's in the finish. I thought, well, have they put it back there or have they put something else in there now? (*He looks round at them craftily.*)

ALBERT (*who has not been listening speaks impatiently*). What's he rambling on about now?

(JAKIE, *glad of the conversation, turns to him eagerly.*)

JAKIE. Your lavatory. I was just saying, I was wondering what you'd got inside this time.

ALBERT. There's nothing in it.

JAKIE. Well, there must be something in it, 'cause I've not been able to get in.

(*There is a short puzzled silence which is broken by* QUEENIE.)

QUEENIE (*as it dawns upon her*). That's where he is!

ALBERT. He's been skulking in that lavatory. (*His voice rises indignantly.*) While I've been chasing all round them brickfields!

QUEENIE (*to* DEANNA, *quietly and ominously*). Go get him.

> (DEANNA *goes out into the yard. It has now grown quite dark and the street light above the yard gives it a sinister quality.* DEANNA *knocks sharply on the lavatory door.*)

DEANNA. Rory! Come on! Come on, let's have you! We know you're in there! (*She pauses.*) My dad knows you're here!

> (DEANNA *waits a moment and then marches back into the house.*)

He won't come.

> (ALBERT *moves angrily towards the door.*)

ALBERT (*grimly*). He'll come.

> (ALBERT *marches out into the yard, leaving the door open behind him.* QUEENIE *stands, arms akimbo, looking towards the door.* ALBERT *kicks the lavatory door.*)

(*viciously.*) Come out! Do you hear me!

> (ALBERT, *unbuckling his belt, moves away from the lavatory and takes up his position at the end of the yard. He stands under the lamp, holding his belt.* HARRY, DEANNA *and* JAKIE *are now, with* QUEENIE, *looking expectantly towards the door.* CHARLES, *with a shrug, begins sawing vigorously at the eagle's neck. After a moment* QUEENIE *turns and watches this operation dully. The others continue looking at the door.* ALBERT *is standing absolutely motionless under the lamp. The head falls from the eagle and as the sawing stops we realize that* RORY *is singing to himself in a cracked and quavering treble. He is singing to bolster up his spirits and occasionally stumbles over a word.*)

RORY (*off*). ". . . O clouds, unfold!

Bring me my chariot of fire!

I will not cease from mental fight,

Nor shall my sword sleep in my hand,

> (*Over the above* QUEENIE *has crossed and picked up the severed head of the eagle. She is cradling it in her hands. As* RORY *continues his voice gathers confidence and he sings the last two lines without any mistake at all.*)

(*Off.*) Till we have built Jerusalem

In England's green and pleasant land."

CURTAIN

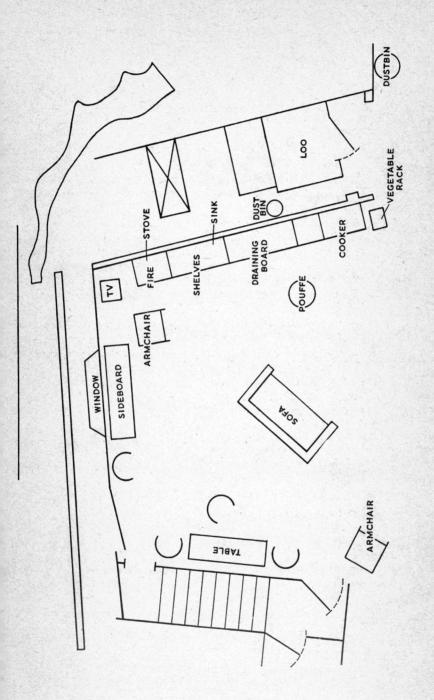

Furniture
As above
On front door CHARLES's coat
On cooker
Frying-pan, kettle
Under cooker
QUEENIE's slippers
On draining board
Dish mop, dish cloth, scourer, large mug, cup, cup and saucer, two tea-spoons, milk bottle with small amount of milk, matches, tea towel
Under draining-board—top shelf
Box of bacon
Plug in sink
In vegetable rack
Cabbage, carrots, potatoes
On shelves—top
Two caddies—one of which containing tea, cash box, cups on hooks
Second
Corn flakes, sugar puffs, jar marmalade, tin milk (open), mug of dripping with knife, sugar, butter, sliced loaf
Third
Knife box, hot-water bottle
Fourth
Plates, saucers, cereal bowls
In fireplace
Poker, fire tongs, shovel, dustpan and brush
On stove
Teapot with tea in
In stove oven
Half piece toast on plate
On armchair D.R.
Comics, newspaper, cushion
On sofa
RORY's shoes D.S., comics U.S., cushion
On television
Radio Times
U.S. of fireplace
Coal scuttle, containing coal
On sideboard
Biscuit tin, blue jug containing biro pen
On table
Tray—on it a dirty cup and saucer, plate, weekend magazine
On armchair D.R.
Form-book, note-book and pencil, cigarette stub, cushion
In R. drawer of sideboard
Toys, space gun, revolver, scrap, cardigan with needle and thread
L. of front door on hook
Lavatory key
On wall R.
Brush set and brush, school photo
In cellar
Sack of staples, cellophane-covered paint-brush, football boots, tea chest

Off R.
   Lectern with one sack over head
   Box of liquorice allsorts
   Newspaper, slum clearance document (JAKIE)
   Fullers earth, straw
   Ledger with rent-book, notification rules
   Three public utilities set in C., fountain pen
   Duffle bag containing football and pair of plimsoles
   Clipboard and pencil
   Carpenter's toolbag containing fireman's axe, saw, oily rag, two sharpeners
   and assorted tools
Off L.
   Carrier bag—in it packet of crisps, two cans of beer
   Blue lectern
   Twenty-nine cans of paint, one large, one small paintbrush, stick and rag
   DEANNA's underclothes, waste-paper basket
   Ten shillings, coppers, newspaper
   One sack
   RORY's Cub uniform
   Woman's Realm magazine
Personal
   DOBSON glasses
   HARRY string

END OF ACT I

Re-set furniture as follows:
   Table to C. of room—four chairs around it
   Sofa to wall R.
   Armchair D.R. to R. of sideboard
   Cellar door ajar
Strike
   Bacon from frying pan (return to box)
   QUEENIE's shoes from under cooker
   QUEENIE's coat from sofa
   Carrier bag from D.L.
   Crisps from shelf
   Weekend magazine
Re-set
   Lectern to lavatory
   Sack to *off* R.
   CHARLES's books to RORY's room
   Pouffe in front of cooker
   Armchair U.L. to red mark
   Cub uniform to top of stairs
   Woman's Realm magazine on floor U.S. of sofa

ACT II

Set
Table
   Packet corn flakes, packet sugar puffs, sliced loaf, butter, jar marmalade,
   sugar bowl, bottle of milk
   R.C.
   Plate and knife, cup and saucer, teapot with hot tea in

L.C.
   Plate and knife, large mug
D.S.
   Plate and knife, cereal bowl with spoon
U.C.
   Plate and knife, cup and saucer
Chair D.S.
   One of RORY's shoes under a comic
   Below on floor space gun and comic
Chair L.
   Tea towel over back, newspaper under D.S. leg
D.S. *arm of sofa*
   DEANNA's underclothes
U.S. *of sofa*
   Dustpan and brush
On sideboard
   Tray, CHARLES's shoes, toys (from drawer), clothes brush
On draining-board
   Half piece of bread D.S. end
In frying-pan
   Crusts, bits of bacon
On floor R. *of table*
   Three crusts

END OF ACT II

Strike
   CHARLES's mug and plate from stove
   Lectern
   Underclothes from stairs
   Toys and comics from cellar
   Chair D.S. of table
   Cushion from armchair U.L.
   Cabbage from vegetable rack
Re-set
   Clothes brush to wall set
   Lavatory key to hook by window
   Oven door of gas cooker ajar
   Tool bag to L. end of sideboard
   Fullers earth on Cub uniform in dustbin
   Pouffe to L. of lectern
Table
   Jar marmalade, milk bottle, 5 plates with two halves buttered bread in one,
   cups, saucers, teapot with tea in, sugar bowl, teaspoon, knife
D.L.
   Lectern—blue—around it D.S. cans of paint on newspaper, one can blue
   paint open, old rag, stick, two paint brushes
   One can of paint just U.R. of the base
R. *of lectern*
   One sack
D.S. *of sofa*
   One sack
Cellar door ajar
On floor D.R.
   R. drawer from sideboard and waste-paper basket